The Hope of the Faithful

THE HOPE OF THE FAITHFUL

Myles Coverdale

A facsimile version of Bishop Myles Coverdale's translation of the German work of Otho Wermullerus, first published circa 1550. This is the Parker Society edition, edited by George Pearson, B.D., and printed in 1846 at The University Press in Cambridge, England.

With an Appendix by Ruth Magnusson Davis

The mission of Baruch House Publishing, founded by editor Ruth Magnusson (Davis), is to bring to the world again the lost works of the early English Reformation. Our main focus is the 1537 Matthew Bible, and our ongoing work is to gently update it for readers today, with reference to the editor's own 1549 edition. The Matthew Bible (MB) was the joint work of William Tyndale (c.1491-1536), Myles Coverdale (c.1487-1569), and John Rogers (c.1500-1555). It is the only English Bible that was bought with blood: both Tyndale and Rogers were burned at the stake for their work. Baruch House also hopes to re-publish individually the best of Myles Coverdale's treatises and small books in attractive, easy-to-read format; this volume is the first such publication.

The publications of Baruch House Publishing include:

The October Testament: The New Testament of the New Matthew Bible (NMB), published in 2016.

The Story of the Matthew Bible: Part 1, That Which We First Received. The true story of the making of the Matthew Bible.

The Story of the Matthew Bible: Part 2, The Scriptures Then and Now. Part 2 of *The Story* tracks the startling changes made to the Matthew Bible since the Reformation and reveals the motivations behind some of them.

More information is on our websites:
www.baruchhousepublishing.com
www.newmatthewbible.org.

THE HOPE OF THE FAITHFUL

Bishop Myles Coverdale, circa 1550. This edition 1846.

From Remains of Myles Coverdale,
published by the Parker Society.

The Society was "Instituted A.D. M.DCCC.XL for the publication of the Works of the Fathers and Early Writers of the Reformed English Church."

EDITED FOR

The Parker Society,

BY THE

REV. GEORGE PEARSON, B.D.

RECTOR OF CASTLE CAMPS,

AND LATE CHRISTIAN ADVOCATE IN THE UNIVERSITY OF CAMBRIDGE.

CAMBRIDGE:

PRINTED AT

THE UNIVERSITY PRESS.

M.DCCC.XLVI.

Copyright © 2020 Ruth Magnusson Davis (Baruch House Publishing)

Minor corrections Jan 2021.

The facsimile of "The Hope of the Faithful" is taken with gratitude from the Parker Society collection *Remains of Myles Coverdale*, published in 1846. The original is in the public domain; however, a considerable amount of work has been invested in preparation of the facsimile for this edition. All rights are reserved. No part of this publication may be reproduced, stored in a retrieval system, or transmitted, in any form or by any means, electronic, mechanical, photocopying, recording, or otherwise, without the prior permission of the publisher.

Contact publisher through the website at www.baruchhousepublishing.com

Cover design by Iryna Spica.

ISBNs Canada:
Paperback 978-1-7771987-0-1
Hardcover 978-1-7771987-1-8
Electronic book 978-1-7771987-2-5
ISBN Amazon (KDP): Paperback 979-8-5814319-7-9

About the cover

The artwork on the front cover is a small detail from a work attributed to Robert Campin, a leading figure in the development of Early Netherlandish painting in the 15th century. This work was commissioned c.1438. Other artists from Campin's workshop may have contributed to certain features of the painting, such as the face of the young woman reading her book. She is Saint Barbara, a Christian martyr believed to have lived in the 3rd century and a popular saint in the Middle Ages. Young Barbara was said to have suffered at the hands of her own father, a wealthy pagan, who executed her for allowing herself to be baptized by a Christian priest.

Table of Contents

Publisher's foreword ... 9

The Hope of the Faithful

Preliminary notices ... 12

Preface "To the Christian Reader" ... 14

THE FIRST PART OF THIS BOOK ... 17
(Chapters I-XII, which discuss the resurrection
and ascension of Christ, with their fruits and benefits)

THE SECOND PART OF THIS BOOK ... 43
(Chapters XIII-XXIII, which discuss our bodies)

THE THIRD PART OF THIS BOOK ... 77
(Chapters XXIV-XXXIII, which discuss the perdition, or
eternal ruin, of the damned, and the salvation of the blessed)

THE TABLE ... 101
(As placed in the original, the table sets out the title
of each chapter of each part of *The Hope of the Faithful*)

*****

The Appendix by R. M. Davis begins at page 105
and contains a separate table of contents.

Publisher's Foreword

The Hope of the Faithful, translated from the German by Myles Coverdale circa 1550, sets forth the traditional doctrine of heaven and hell. It was written to refute those who denied that there is an eternal life and an eternal damnation.

In the years 1547-1553, during the reign of young Edward VI, there was a burst of Protestant printing in England, which ceased only after Queen Mary ascended the throne. Almost three hundred years later, the Parker Society undertook to republish some of the works of the early English Reformation, from the time of Henry VIII to King Edward. The Parker Society edition of *Remains/Hope of the Faithful* refers the reader to a foreword to another of Bishop Coverdale's translations for additional information. That foreword says,

> This Treatise [*A Spiritual and Most Precious Pearl*] is a translation from the German of Otho Wermullerus, or Vuerdmullerus, an eminent scholar and divine of Zurich, contemporary of Bishop Coverdale. Of this we are informed by Hugh Singleton, in the preface to an edition published by him after Coverdale's death, in which he states that, in consequence of some spurious editions, which had been published in his name, "he had thought it good to set it forth again according to the true copy of that translation that he received at the hands of M. Doctor Milo Coverdale"; At whose hand he received also the copies of three other works of Wermullerus. The names of these other books are: first, *A Treatise on Death;*

the second, *Of Justification*; and the third, *Of the Hope of the Faithful*.

This work was first sent forth under the especial patronage of the Protector Somerset in 1550, on the conclusion of his troubles at that period, and under the circumstances stated in the preface prefixed to this edition by the Protector himself. This fact is also mentioned in the title page to this edition, in which it is said to have been "sett forth by the moste honorable Lorde, the duke his grace of Somerset, as appeareth by hys Epystle set before the same." But no mention is made either of Wermullerus or Coverdale; the fact of its being a translation from the former being, as far as appears, first noticed in the edition of Hugh Singleton. Copies of this interesting edition are found in the library of the British Museum, and in that of the Dean and Chapter of Peterborough.

The mission of Baruch House Publishing is to publish more of Coverdale's translations and his own works in easy-to-read facsimile editions. These will include *A Spiritual and Most Precious Pearl* and *Treatise on Death*.

Ruth Magnusson Davis, 2020

This facsimile edition has been carefully prepared to remove all possible imperfections. Any remaining imperfections are a necessary part of the character of the work.

THE
HOPE OF THE FAITHFUL.

The Hope of the Faythfull,

declaringe breefely and clearely the Resurrection of
our Lord Jesus Christ past, and of our true
essentiall bodies to come: and playnely con-
futing the chiefe errors that habe sprong
thereof out of the Scripture and Doc-
tors. With an ebident probatiō
that there is an eternall life of
the faithful, and eberlasting
damnation of the
wicked.

[THE HOPE OF THE FAITHFUL.

This is the third of the treatises of Otho Wermullerus, or Vierdmullerus, translated by Bishop Coverdale; for an account of which the reader is referred to the preface to the Spiritual Pearl. Of this work there are copies of the edition printed by Hugh Singleton in 1579 in the libraries of Christ Church, Oxford, and of Trinity college, Dublin. The present edition is printed from a copy of the old edition without date in the Swiss angular type, (exactly resembling that in which the preceding treatise is printed, and both of them probably under the immediate superintendence of Coverdale himself,) in the possession of George Offor, Esq.]

PREFACE.

TO THE CHRISTIAN READER,

GRACE AND PEACE.

EVERY man must needs confess, that this is now a lamentable time, in the which the world is not only unquieted with wars, dearth, sickness, and such like; but also standeth ever more and more in greater peril, through vices every where bearing the sway: so that it is to be feared, if we banish them not the sooner, we and our posterity shall yet come into far greater sorrow, than we are already wrapped in. For if one should barely, and without all rhetorical amplifications, rehearse only the great pomp, vain glory, riot, fornication, open idolatry, perjury, &c. of mighty men and rulers, which waste the world miserably, the space even of many days would scarce be any thing sufficient thereunto.

And what heaps of wickedness private persons do add unto the same, all wise men can ponder by themselves. For if we go into our own bosoms, we find that we altogether will wholly fashion and frame our lives after the world; seeking vain pomp and private commodity for our own lust, with sure shame and public discommodity to others' loss.

Which all are undoubted tokens, that the law and love of God is little esteemed among us; which with grievous threats forbiddeth the aforesaid and other vices, by strait commandment forcing, and sure rewards alluring us to the contrary dealing. Neither may we think, but that such vices daily will increase, until the time they overwhelm us, except, the contempt of God's law set apart, (being the only sufficient well-spring of all wickedness, for which the wrath of God is enkindled and his bitter curses fall upon us,) the same would be had in greater price and reverence. For why? what godliness can be hoped for of them which hold nothing of God, the only fountain of goodness, and laugh his word to scorn, of whom we can know nothing but is there shewed us, save the small knowledge there is of beholding of the creatures; which nevertheless declareth rather, that there is a God, than what he is, and how he will be pleased? And, though all the scriptures serve us to enjoy God's blessings, yet as in a compound medicine all the simples being wholesome, some one may less be spared than the other; so the article of resurrection, clear and oft inculcated in scripture, is most available, so that it is known all vices swarm and roost in us. For we not considering our end, wherein salvation and life standeth, or pains prepared for the accursed, will but stain ourselves in voluptuousness. For who knoweth but the flesh in this life, why should he not think as good take it, as leave it, and best to make the most of that which at last ceaseth? In this case the Ethnics being, said: "Live merrily while ye be in the world, and eat we and drink we lustily; to-morrow we shall die:" which all the epicures protest openly, and the Italian *atheoi* in like practice; and no worse man than a pope in our days hath given the like definitive sentence among his court divines of the soul's immortality[1]: the story is known. Contrariwise the learned in God's word, knowing that this life is a death from sin, and a way to the life to come, which Christ with his cross hath opened unto them, for desire thereof run forth in the race of godliness, assured of the reward; since Christ therefore, by doing death battle, that we might live, hath broken her bonds, and risen again. For goods are not the possessor's, as the philosopher saith, and Christ alludeth in

[[1] Allusion is probably made to Leo X.; who has often been charged not only with holding infidel opinions, but also with giving utterance to them. Compare with what is here stated, what is written concerning Leo by Waterland, in his Charge on *Christianity defended against Infidelity*; Works, Vol. VIII. p. 77. Ed. 1823: also the remarks which are made on his character by Seckendorf, *Commentarius de Lutheranismo*, (Lib. I. sect. 47. § CXVIII. Vol. I. p. 190,) who thus gives his opinion of Leo: Hæc et alia ad mores Leonis pertinentia *Varillasius* nuper in *Arcana historia Florentina* prodidit, ex quibus et ex silentio *Pallavicini* judicium *Pauli Veneti* de Pontifice hoc confirmatur, quod duobus maximis vitiis laboraverit ignorantia religionis, et impietate, sive atheismo. See Illyr. Flac. Catalog. Test. Genev. 1608. col. 2103. Also Bale, Pageant of Popes, Lond. 1574. fol. 179.]

the parable of the two strong men, but the more valiant man's. Wherefore, gentle reader, I having this little, but absolute work of Christ's and our resurrection, and that there is an eternal life and damnation, wherein the devil hath sore assaulted the church by men (this only excepted) of great authority and learning, thought it my duty to put it in print, not keeping that private, which might do such good common. The matter is plain in scripture; yet learn we better things called in question, and forced to us by reason: wherefore not to stir up God's grace in us by embracing such treatises, were to tempt God, and extinct the Spirit.

 For the scholar learneth of his schoolfellow, what he perceived not by his more learned master, and understandeth him ever after the better; and so men further one another
in scripture: which, as I mean in printing, if thou desire
in reading, the Lord, no nay, shall grant our request,
which giveth blessings plenteously to all such
as ask it constantly. To whom give
honour and thanks from heart,
for the good that thou
reapest in his crea-
tures. Farewell.

THE

FIRST PART OF THIS BOOK,

ENTITLED

THE HOPE OF THE FAITHFUL,

WHICH ENTREATETH OF THE RESURRECTION AND
ASCENSION OF CHRIST, WITH THE FRUIT
AND COMMODITY THEREOF.

CHAPTER I.

THE CONTENTS OF THIS BOOK, AND THE AUTHOR'S
PURPOSE.

CONSIDERING that by the evangelists and by all the apostles there is nothing written more diligently, than touching the resurrection of our Lord Jesus Christ, my purpose is somewhat more largely to talk of the same, and of the glorious ascension of his body into heaven: item, of the resurrection and ascension of our own bodies, of the damnation of unbelievers, of the hope and eternal life of the blessed. And this I mind to do only unto the honour, laud, and praise of our Lord Jesus Christ; that the mystery of the holy gospel may be set forth and opened to the commodity and edifying of the faithful, and that of every man it may be plainly understood, how great things are prepared and given us of Christ. This matter also doth specially belong to the declaration of the holy gospel; forasmuch as the best state of the gospel is contained and taught therein. Therefore if I write aught herein more largely, I do nothing that concerneth not my purpose. Yet I intend also to keep a measure, and not to open every thing that hereof might be written, but only that which is chiefest and most necessary of all.

CHAPTER II.

THAT THE LORD VERILY AROSE WITH HIS BODY.

THAT our Lord Jesus Christ with his own very true body did verily arise from the dead, it shall be expedient before all things to testify and prove. Therefore let the first witness, even the Lord Jesus Christ himself, come forth now, and bear us record out of the prophets concerning his true resurrection: "Like as Jonas," saith he, "was three days and three nights in the whale's belly, so shall the Son of man be three days and three nights in the heart of the earth." Now did not the fish cast up to the dry land any other for Jonas, but even the same Jonas himself, whom he had swallowed. Therefore the very same true body of the Lord also, that was buried, arose again. Which thing the holy apostle Paul minding perfectly to express, said: "First of all I delivered unto you, or taught you, that which I received; how that Christ died for our sins according to the scriptures; and that he was buried, and that he rose again the third day according to the scriptures." [Matt. xii.] [1 Cor. xv.]

Lo, what can be spoken more evident and plain? He that died for our sins, and was buried, even he himself the very same rose also again. Of this now it followeth, that the very true substantial body of our Lord did rise again; for even the same died, and was buried. But to the intent that it might the sooner be believed, Paul, the holy teacher, declareth furthermore, that he speaketh thus according to the contents of scripture, and that the same was taught in the scriptures afore, meaning undoubtedly the law and the prophets.

Nevertheless we will now bring forth the true and evident testimonies of the angels, who in Mark, Luke, and Matthew, speak unto the women that came to the sepulchre: "Ye seek Jesus of Nazareth, him that was crucified. Why seek ye the living among the dead? He is risen, he is not here. Behold the place where they had laid him. Remember, how he spake unto you, while he was yet in Galilee, saying, that the Son of man must be delivered into the hands of sinful men, and be crucified, and the third day rise again. There- [Matt. xxviii. Mark xvi. Luke xxiv.]

fore go quickly and tell this to his disciples, that he is risen from the dead. And behold, he shall go before you into Galilee; there shall ye see him, as he himself told you."

These are the words of the angels, which, if all circumstances be thoroughly well considered, do plainly declare, that the very true body of the Lord did verily arise from the dead. The women come and seek the body of the Lord, desiring to anoint it; therefore the question is touching the body of Christ. The angels also speak of the true body of Christ, and make answer, saying, "Ye seek Jesus of Nazareth;" whereunto they add distinctly, "him that was crucified." Now are we sure, that his very true body was crucified, and died. He, say they namely, that died, even Jesus of Nazareth, the same is become alive again. "Why seek ye the living among the dead?" The Lord died of a truth; but death must not have dominion over him, neither must his body putrefy or corrupt, as other men's bodies do; according as holy David said before: "Aforehand I saw God Psal. xvi. always before me; for he is on my right hand, that I should not be moved. Therefore did my heart rejoice, and my tongue was glad; moreover my flesh also shall rest in hope; because thou wilt not leave my soul in hell, neither wilt thou suffer thy Holy One to see corruption. Thou hast shewed me the ways of life, thou shalt make me full of joy with thy countenance; and at thy right hand there is pleasure for evermore." These words extend wholly unto Christ, according as the two excellent apostles, namely, Peter in the Acts ii. xiii. second, and Paul in the thirteenth of the Acts, do declare. Out of the angels' words also is it come into the articles of the Creed, as we all confess with these words, "HE ROSE AGAIN FROM THE DEAD." This word, "from the dead," doth truly express the death and resurrection after this sense: He died, as other men also do, according to the law of nature; and even in the same flesh, which he therefore took upon him that he might die, received the immortality, and took it unto him again. Therefore, say the angels, "he is risen again." But that thing riseth not up, which fell not afore; therefore even the same body of Christ, that fell to death, is from death risen up again.

Moreover, they name also the place where he was laid, to express perfectly, that the very true body was risen, saying:

"Behold the place where they laid him." The mortal body of the Lord hath his certain place, yea, his own place, (that the logicians call *ubi*, that is to say, where,) in the which he was laid; and as he now is become immortal, he hath his own place again. For if the body that was raised up were every where, then had not the angels said: "Behold the place where they laid him." Yea, they had not been able to shew any one place, where he was not; for the immortal body must be every where. But now they shew a place, in which the immortal body was not, and that with plain express words, saying: "He is not here." Of this now it followeth, that the body of Christ, which is but in one place, did verily rise again. In the gospel of St John also the sepulchre-clothes wherein the Lord was wrapped (as the head-cloth and that which was about his body) are mentioned as strong testimonies of the body risen up; which clothes Peter and John did perfectly see.

Furthermore, the angels prove his very true resurrection out of the word of God, and say: "Remember what he said unto you, while he was yet in Galilee: The Son of man must be delivered into the hands of sinful men," &c. With these words will they instruct us, that the Son of man, in a very true body, is truly risen again. They say moreover: "Go quickly, tell the disciples, that he is risen from death." Now was the body dead, and, as all men's bodies that die, laid in the grave. And even the same body was made immortal, and rose again from the dead. "He shall go before you into Galilee," yea, before you shall he go with a true body, that moveth from one place unto another; "there," as in a certain place, "shall ye see him." "Ye shall see him," I say; for with a visible and palpable body is he risen, as ye are told by the Lord himself, who can neither lie nor deceive.

CHAPTER III.

APPEARINGS OF THE BODY RAISED UP.

HEREUNTO extend the manifold appearings, or open-shewings of Christ, mentioned by the evangelists. In Mark it is written thus: "When Jesus was risen early the first ^{Mark xvi.} day after the Sabbath, he appeared first to Mary Magdalen;" to whom in the gospel of St John he saith: "Go to my ^{John xx.} brethren, and tell them, I go up to my Father and your Father, to my God and your God. Now when she came to the disciples, she told them that she had seen the Lord, and that he had spoken such things unto her." In Matthew he meeteth the women, and saith: "All hail. Fear not: go ^{Matt. xxviii.} and tell my brethren, that they go into Galilee; there shall they see me." In holy St Luke is mention made of two appearings: the first, when he shewed himself to the two that went to Emaus, and opened unto them the true re- ^{Luke xxiv.} surrection of his body; the second, when they were gone again from Jerusalem, they came to the disciples, minding to shew them, and to give them to understand, what they had seen and heard. Then prevented they them, and said: "The ^{Luke xxiv.} Lord is truly risen indeed, and hath appeared unto Simon." "Now while they were talking of such things among themselves, Jesus stood in the midst of them, and said, Peace be unto you. But when they saw him, they were sore afraid, thinking that they had seen a spirit, or some other vision. Then said the Lord unto them, Why are ye troubled, and why do thoughts arise in your hearts? behold my hands and my feet."

CHAPTER IV.

THE BODY OF CHRIST ROSE AGAIN, NOT A SPIRIT, BUT A TRUE BODY.

Now, that no man should think it to be another body, which he had not afore his resurrection, he addeth thereto immediately: "It is even I myself; handle me, and see; a spirit hath not flesh and bones, as ye see me have. And with that he shewed them his hands and his feet."

With this evident testimony of the Lord was St Augus- ^{De Agone Christiano.} tine moved boldly to say, that "they ought not to be heard, ^{cap. 24.} which deny the body of the Lord to have risen again, as it was laid in the sepulchre. For if it were not so, he would not have said to his disciples after the resurrection: 'Handle me and see; for a spirit hath not flesh and bones, as ye see me have.' Now is it as much as to rob God of his honour, if any man would think that the Lord, who is the truth itself, had, in anything that he spake, not said the truth[1]."

Thomas was not there, when the Lord shewed himself alive unto his disciples; but when he came again, they told him with great joy what they had seen and heard. Nevertheless he thought it had not been as they spake, and he said: "Except I see in his hands the print of the nails, and put my fingers into the holes of them, and my hand into his side, I will not believe it. Therefore after eight days, when the disciples were assembled together again, and Thomas with them, Jesus cometh in, while the doors were shut, and standeth in the midst among them, and saith, Peace be unto you. Afterwards said he unto Thomas, Reach hither thy finger, and behold my hands; put thy hand here also, and lay it in my side; and be not faithless but believing. Thomas answered and said unto him, My Lord, and my God." For St Paul also, in the first chapter of the epistle to the Romans, doth out of the resurrection of the Lord prove the Godhead thus: "Which was born of the seed of David after the flesh, and evidently declared to be the Son of God after the Spirit that sanctifieth, and by that he rose again from the dead;" namely, Jesus Christ our Lord. What can be spoken more plain, more evident, or more certain? For freely did the Lord set before their eyes his body which was hanged upon the cross, that they might see it and handle it. For the body was pierced with nails, and marred with the prints thereof. Out of this now it followeth, that the Lord with his true body did verily rise again, and was not a spirit. And further, the Lord also sheweth himself unto the seven, which then were in Galilee, fishing at the Sea of Tiberias. The evangelist addeth likewise thereunto, that it was not expedient for any

[1 Nec eos audiamus, qui negant tale corpus Domini resurrexisse, quale positum est in monumento. Si enim tale non fuisset, non ipse dixisset post resurrectionem discipulis, Palpate et videte, quoniam spiritus ossa et carnem non habet, sicut me videtis habere. Sacrilegum est enim credere, Dominum nostrum, cum ipse sit veritas, in aliquo fuisse mentitum. August. De Agone Christiano. cap. 24. Opera, Tom. III. p. 74. F. ed. Paris. 1541.]

of the disciples to ask him who he was; for they knew that it was the Lord. In the twenty-eighth chapter of Matthew, the eleven apostles "saw the Lord, and worshipped him," as Matt. xxviii. it is declared afore. Some think, that the same was the excellent appearing that Paul speaketh of, saying: "Afterwards 1 Cor. xv. was he seen of more than five hundred brethren at once, of whom many are alive this day, but some are asleep," or dead. And in the same place doth the apostle make mention yet of two more appearings, saying: "After this was he seen of James, then of all the apostles, and last of all he was seen of me, as of one that was born out of due time."

Luke the Evangelist, in the beginning of the Acts of the Apostles, hath in manner collected all the probations together. "The Lord," saith he, "shewed himself alive unto Acts i. his apostles after his passion; and that by many tokens, appearing unto them forty days, and speaking of the kingdom of God." St Peter also, instructing Cornelius in the faith of Christ, said: "We are witnesses of all things which Matt. x. he did in the land of the Jews, and at Jerusalem; whom they slew and hanged on a tree: him God raised up the third day, and shewed him openly, not to all the people, but unto us witnesses chosen before of God, for that intent, which did eat and drink with him after he arose from death." With these plain probations and testimonies, as I suppose it, it is evidently declared and sufficiently shewed, that our Lord Jesus Christ, with his own very true body which hanged on the cross, did verily rise from the dead. As touching the glorification, I shall speak thereof, when I come to the resurrection of the bodies; and there will I shew more, that the glorification doth nothing minish the verity or truth of the body. Read the sixth chapter.

CHAPTER V.

THE FRUIT OF THE RESURRECTION OF CHRIST.

Now will I declare the occasion, why I have with such diligence and so earnestly pressed on to this, that Jesus Christ with his true body did truly rise again: that is, how profitable and necessary it is so to believe, and what fruit the true resurrection of Christ doth bring and engender unto us. And albeit that hereof, as of a plentiful treasure, much might be spoken, yet will I comprehend it all in a short sum. Though we be complete and made perfect through the death of Christ, while the just judgment of God is satisfied, the curse taken away, and the penalty recom-

1 Peter i. pensed and paid; yet saith Peter, that "we are born again through the resurrection of Jesus Christ unto a living hope." For like as Christ with his resurrection overcame death, so standeth also the triumph and victory of our faith in the resurrection of Christ. Therefore through his death is sin taken away, by his resurrection is righteousness brought again. For how could he with his death have delivered us from death, if he himself had of death been overcome? or how could he have obtained the victory for us, if he had been destroyed in the battle himself? Therefore through death is death discomfited, and with the resurrection is life to us restored.

1 Cor. xv. Hereof cometh it that Paul saith: "If Christ be not risen, then is your faith in vain, and ye are yet still in your sins; and so they that be asleep in Christ are lost;" and to the

Rom. iv. Romans: "Christ," saith he, "was delivered up for our sins, and rose again for our justification."

Rom. x. Hereunto cometh it also that he writeth in the tenth chapter: "If ye confess the Lord Jesus with thy mouth, and believe in thine heart, that God raised him from the dead, thou shalt be saved."

Phil. iii. To the Philippians he saith moreover: "I count all things but loss for the excellent knowledge sake of Jesus Christ."

Out of all this is there yet another thing concluded, namely, that not only life is restored unto us, but also that in the resurrection of the Lord the immortality of the soul is grounded fast and sure. For so saith the Lord himself

John xi. in the Gospel: "I am the resurrection and the life: he that believeth on me, though he were dead, he shall live; and whosoever liveth and believeth on me shall never die."

Yet another fruit also receive we out of the resurrection of the Lord, namely, that we are assured and out of doubt, even as if we had received writing and seal thereof, that our own bodies likewise shall rise from death; forasmuch as in the true resurrection of the body of Christ our resurrection hath a fast and immoveable ground. For Paul saith: "Christ rose from the dead, and is become the first-fruits of them that sleep. For by one man came death, and by one man came the resurrection of the dead. For as by Adam all die, so by Christ shall all be made alive. But every one in his own order: the first is Christ, then they that are Christ's." Now he that is the first cannot be alone; the head also shall not forsake the members. Seeing then that Christ the head is risen, it must needs follow, that we also as members must rise again. For even in the same place doth Paul conclude: "If the dead rise not again, then is not Christ risen again." 1 Cor. xv.

And finally, out of the words of the holy apostle Paul we learn, that through the ensample of Christ that was raised up, we are not only provoked to take upon us a new life; but that we also, through the power of Christ, are renewed, that we might lead an innocent and holy life. And thus have I briefly comprehended and declared the principal fruits of the resurrection of the Lord. Rom. vi. Coloss. iii.

CHAPTER VI.

OF THE TRUE ASCENSION OF THE LORD'S BODY, THAT AROSE A BODY, AND NO SPIRIT; AND OF HIS PLACE WHITHER HE WENT TO BE IN.

MOREOVER it shall be expedient to know, to what place the true body of the Lord was carried, or came; whether it was laid in the earth again, or vanished away, or turned into the nature of the Godhead, or otherwise changed into a spirit. In this point we affirm thus. The right old christian faith, the upright holy scripture, and the ancient doctrine of the christian church, doth teach, hold, and confess, that Jesus Christ, very God and man, hath not laid away, nor mixed together, nor yet put off his natures, the Godhead and the manhood; but that he keepeth still both the natures in their properties unblemished, and that he ascended up to heaven very true God and man. For so we acknowledge and confess in the Creed: "HE ASCENDED UP TO HEAVEN."

<small>Mark xvi.</small> We find also in the Gospel of Mark: "So then when the Lord had spoken unto them, he was received into heaven, <small>Ruffinus.</small> and sitteth at the right hand of God." Item, Ruffinus, an old writer, who hath declared the articles of the faith, saith: "He ascended into the heavens, not thither where the Word that is God was not afore, (for he was ever still in heaven, and continued in his Father;) but thither where the Word that became man sat not afore[1]." Yet will we declare this more plainly out of the Gospel of Luke, where it is written <small>Luke xxiv.</small> thus: "And he led them out into Bethany, and lift up his hands, and blessed them: and it came to pass, as he blessed them, he departed from them, and was carried up into heaven."

Now if thou ponder everything here thoroughly, thou must needs acknowledge, and being overcome with the truth thou must needs confess, that the very true body of the Lord was not laid away, neither turned into the nature of the Godhead[2]; but he a very true man, who at one time is but in one place, ascended and was taken up into heaven, as into one place: "He led them out," saith he. Who, I pray thee? Even the Lord Jesus Christ, which until then, by the space of forty days had in very deed truly shewed himself unto his disciples, that he was risen from the dead with a very true essential body,—even he, the very same that had taken unto him a true body, led his disciples out unto Bethany, and from thence brought he them further to mount Olivet; and in the same place lifting up his hands, (no doubt bodily and human hands, yea, with the prints and tokens of the wounds,) he blessed them, namely, his disciples, that is, he saluted them, as the manner is of those that take their leave of us; and so departed he from them, and set his body corporally in heaven, as in one place. For afterwards it followeth yet more plain: "he departed from them," that is,

[1 Ascendit ergo ad cœlos, non ubi Verbum Deus ante non fuerat; quippe qui erat semper in cœlis, et manebat in Patre; sed ubi Verbum caro factum ante non fuerat. Ruffini Expositio in Symbolum Apostolicum apud Cypriani Opera, edit. Fell; also Opuscula, p. 185, ed. 1580.]

[2 Some account of the Apellitæ, and of other persons who held heretical opinions on our Lord's ascension, are found in bishop Pearson, *On the Creed*. Art. VI.]

he was carried into heaven. For to be carried may here be spoken only of the body; and in such sort departed he from them, that his body was from the earth taken up into heaven.

And though all this be evident and plain in itself, yet by the Evangelist Luke in the Acts of the Apostles is it set forth and opened more manifestly. So afore all things he testifieth, that the Lord arose with his own true body, and that by the space of forty days with many tokens and evidences he plainly proved and declared his resurrection unto the disciples; and immediately he addeth thereunto, and even the very same body was taken up into heaven: "for when he had spoke these things," saith he, "while they beheld him, he was taken up on high, and a cloud received him up out of their sight." So the Lord was taken up, yea, even in their eye-sight was he taken up on high; so that a cloud received his very true body away from the sight of their eyes. I beseech you, what can be more aptly or more conveniently spoken of an essential body? Acts i.

It followeth further in the evangelist Luke: "And while they looked stedfastly up towards heaven, as he went, (mark that well), behold, two men stood by them in white apparel, which also said, Ye men of Galilee, why stand ye gazing up into heaven? This same Jesus, who is taken up from you into heaven, shall so come, even as ye have seen him go into heaven." Wherefore our Lord Jesus is departed up into heaven with his own true essential body, yea, even with the same which he raised up from death. For even with the same very true human body shall he come again unto judgment, according as the Lord himself said, and the prophet Zachary, whose words St John allegeth: "They shall look on him whom they have pierced." Matt. xxvi.
Zech. xii.
John xix.

Thus, I trust, is sufficiently proved and declared, that the Lord Jesus with his own very true body, which he raised from death, is gone up into heaven. But to the intent that no man mistake this word, *heaven*, or otherwise imagine anything that is dark or not understood, whereby the simple, being in error, may scarce know at the last where heaven is, or where Christ hath his dwelling; it shall therefore be needful briefly to declare, what the heaven is, and that the Lord with his own true body doth dwell in heaven, as in one place: for heaven is a certain assured place, and not only a name and declaration of the estate and being in heaven. Therefore when it is said, "Christ is gone up into heaven," it is not so much as only to say, he hath taken upon him an heavenly estate or being; but also, he dwelleth bodily in heaven, as in one place.

CHAPTER VII.

THE DIVERS SIGNIFICATIONS OF THIS WORD HEAVEN, AS IT IS USED IN SCRIPTURE.

THIS word, *heaven*, in the scripture is used divers and sundry ways. First, for the whole firmament, which is called the heavenly host, or beautiful apparel of the heavens. Hereof hast thou record in the eighth and nineteenth Psalms. *[Psalm viii. xix.]* It is taken also for the air, which is above us, as the prophet saith: "He covereth the heaven with clouds, to prepare rain for the earth." *[Psalm cxlvi. cxlvii.]* Hereof cometh it, that the fowls which fly in the air are called fowls or birds of heaven, that is to say, birds in the air. The heaven also is used for a seat, habitation, or dwelling, as: "The Lord hath prepared his seat in heaven;" and, "Ye shall not swear by heaven, for it is God's seat:" *[Psalm ciii. civ. Matt. v.]* and though God be infinite, and cannot be compassed about with any place, as the most wise Salomon said: "The heavens and the heavens of all heavens are not able to contain thee, and how should then this house do it, that I have builded?" *[1 Kings viii.]* yet the scripture calleth the heaven that is above us a dwelling of God; which dwelling is ordained for all faithful and virtuous believers, and is named the heaven. This doth Paul witness, saying: "We know that if our earthly mansion of this dwelling were destroyed, we have a building of God, an habitation not made with hands, but eternal in heaven." *[2 Cor. v.]* There is now heaven taken for the kingdom of God, for the kingdom of the Father, or joy and eternal life, which is peace and rest. The heaven, I say, is a seat and dwelling of the faithful, or blessed believers; a determinate place also, into which the Lord Jesus was received, when he was taken up into the heaven. And this doth the scripture plainly declare unto us, namely, that

above us there is a certain determinate place prepared for
us. For Luke saith: "He was received up on high, and a Acts i.
cloud took him up away out of their sight." Item: "And
while they looked stedfastly up towards heaven, the angels
said, This same Jesus, which is taken away from you into
heaven, shall so come, even as ye have seen him go into
heaven." Who is so ignorant now, that he wotteth not
where heaven is, or the clouds, or into which heaven the
apostles looked so stedfastly? Besides this, the holy apostle
Paul saith: "Also our conversation, free burghership, or Phil. iii.
dwelling, is in heaven, from whence we look for the Saviour,
even the Lord Jesus." Lo, "in heaven," saith the apostle,
"is our dwelling." In which heaven, I pray you? Even in
the same, whence we look for the Saviour. Now is it
evident, from whence we wait and look, seeing that the
apostle saith again: "We which shall live and remain, shall 1 Thess. iv.
be caught up with him also in the clouds to meet the Lord
in the air, and so shall we ever be with the Lord." He
saith also in another place: "If ye be risen again with Col. iii.
Christ, then seek those things which are above, where Christ
sitteth at the right hand of God." And therefore is the
Lord Jesus gone up into the heaven that is above us, namely,
into that sure certain place, which is prepared for the blessed.

And in the same heaven, as in a sure certain place, doth
Christ now dwell bodily.

Of this opinion also was holy Augustine, as indeed it is
right and agreeable unto holy scripture. His words are
found in the book *Ad Dardanum de præsentia Dei*[1]. Holy
Fulgentius, in the second book that he wrote unto king Tra- Fulgentius.
simundus, is earnest to bring every man unto this understanding, that the human kind and nature of Christ, which
now dwelleth in heaven, is circumscribed and in one place[2].

[1 Noli itaque dubitare, ibi nunc esse hominem Jesum Christum,
unde venturus est; memoriterque recole, et fideliter tene Christianam
confessionem; quoniam resurrexit a mortuis, ascendit in cœlum, sedet
ad dexteram Patris, nec aliunde quam inde venturus est ad vivos
mortuosque judicandos. Et sic venturus est, illa angelica voce testante,
quemadmodum ire visus est in cœlum; id est, in eadem carnis forma
et substantia, cui profecto immortalitatem dedit, naturam non abstulit. August. Epistolæ. Ad Dardan. Epist. lvii. Opera, Tom. ii. p. 56.
M. ed. Par. 1541.]

[2 Fulgentii Opera. pp. 88, &c. ed. 1684, particularly cap. xviii.]

<small>Vigilius.</small> With him also accordeth uniformly the holy martyr Vigilius[1]; whose testimony I will now omit, and come again to the holy scripture.

The scripture, minding to shew what is become of the body that rose again from death and ascended up, and where he hath his dwelling, saith simply and plainly: "He sitteth at the right hand of God, the Father Almighty." Thus now is the body of Christ come to the right hand of God; there sitteth he. But here it shall be expedient to declare what the right hand of God is, and what it is to sit at God's right hand.

CHAPTER VIII.

WHAT GOD'S RIGHT HAND IS, AND TO WHOM IT IS REFERRED.

FIRST, the right hand of God is not referred unto God himself, but unto men that are on the right hand. So that first the right hand of God doth signify the eternal salvation, and the place of those that be saved. This did holy Augustine teach, whose words I may well allege; forasmuch as he also doth confirm and prove his opinion by the divine and holy scriptures. In his book *De Agone Christiano* he saith: <small>Augustinus De Agone Christiano. cap. 26.</small> "We ought not to hear them that deny the Son to sit at the right hand of God. For they say, Hath God the Father also a right or left side, as bodies have? Neither do we understand that of the Father. For with no bodily proportion can God be described or comprehended. As for the right hand of the Father, it is nothing else but the eternal salvation, which he shall give to all godly and faithful believers. In like manner is the left hand rightly taken for the everlasting damnation that shall come upon the unbelievers. So that not of God, but of the creatures, it must be expounded what is written of the right or left hand. For even the body of Christ also, which is the church, shall come to the right hand, that is, unto salvation, as the apostle <small>Ephes. ii.</small> saith to the Ephesians: 'He hath raised us up together with him, and made us sit together with him among them of

---

[[1] Vigilii Opera. Contra Varimadum, Lib. I. cap. 37. ed. 1564.]

heaven.' For though our bodies as yet be not there, our hope nevertheless is there already². "

The same holy Augustine saith also further in the book *De Fide et Symbolo:* "By the right hand," saith he, "must be understood the highest salvation, where righteousness, peace, and joy is: like as the goats also shall be set on the left hand; that is, by reason of their sins and wickedness, they shall come into great calamity, trouble, and misery³." All these are the words of holy Augustine.

<small>De Fide et Symbolo. cap. 7</small>

CHAPTER IX.

WHAT IT IS TO SIT AT THE RIGHT HAND OF GOD. HOW CHRIST SITTETH THERE, AND WHAT HE DOETH.

AND thus now to sit at the right hand of God, is even as much as to be in rest, that is to say, all wickedness and misery set aside, to live in a godly life, and to be partaker of eternal joy.

Now that this word, *to sit*, is used in scripture for rest, these places declare. In the fourth book of Moses it is written thus: "Shall your brethren go to war, and would <small>Num. xxxii.</small>

[² Nec eos audiamus, qui negant ad dexteram Patris sedere Filium. Dicunt enim, Numquid Deus Pater habet latus dexterum aut sinistrum, sicut corpora? Nec nos hoc de Deo sentimus: nulla enim forma corporis Deus definitur et concluditur. Sed dextera Patris est beatitudo perpetua, quæ sanctis datur; sicut sinistra ejus rectissime dicitur miseria perpetua, quæ impiis datur: ut non in ipso Deo, sed in creaturis, hoc modo quo diximus intelligatur dextera et sinistra; quia et corpus Christi, quod est ecclesia, in ipsa dextera, hoc est, in ipsa beatitudine futurum est, sicut apostolus dixit, Quia et simul nos suscitavit, et simul nos sedere fecit in cœlestibus. Quamvis enim corpus nostrum nondum ibi sit, tamen spes nostra ibi jam est. August. De Agon. Christian. cap. 26. Opera, Tom. III. p. 174. G.]

[³ Credimus etiam, quod sedet ad dexteram Patris: nec ideo tamen quasi humana forma circumscriptum esse Deum Patrem arbitrandum est, ut de illo cogitantibus dexterum aut sinistrum latus animo occurrat.......Ad dexteram igitur intelligendum est dictum esse in summa beatitudine, ubi et justitia, et pax, et gaudium est: sicut ad sinistram hædi constituuntur, id est, in miseria, propter iniquitates et labores et cruciatus. Id. de Fide et Symbolo. cap. 7. Opera, Tom. III. p. 33. F.]

<small>Micah iv.</small> ye sit here?" and in Micah, "Every one shall sit under his vine and fig-tree." Many more such places there be. Wherefore now, when the scripture saith, that the Lord Jesus sitteth at the right hand of his Father, it understandeth it chiefly of his human nature which he took upon him, that the same, being discharged and free from all travail and misery of man, is now all in joy, and partaker of the kingdom everlasting.

<small>Ruffinus.</small> Thus saith also Ruffinus in his exposition of the Creed: "To sit at the right hand of the Father is convenient for the manhood received, which is received through a mystery. For to ascribe it to the divine nature is unseemly, as though it had a seat in heaven; but of the human nature it is properly understood and spoken[1]."

<small>Acts ii. iii.</small> And the like yet did holy Saint Peter teach afore Ruffinus's time, as it is to see in the Acts of the Apostles.

But now might one ask, What doeth the Son at the right hand of the Father? must he always sit there, and be as much as made fast and bound unto it?

Answer. The Lord Jesus, after his human nature that he took upon him, and which he put not from him in heaven, hath now eternal joy with his elect; he, as the head with his members, ruling and reigning with all faithful believers for evermore. Whereof we shall speak more afterward.

A very superfluous and unprofitable question also is it, when one will so curiously inquire and know, what God doeth in heaven.

For God will only teach us with his holy word, that he liveth and ruleth eternally in the glory of his heavenly <small>De Fide et Symbolo. cap. 6.</small> Father. Holy Augustine saith also in the book *De Fide et Symbolo*: "To go about for to seek and inquire, where and how the body of our Lord is in heaven, it is a point of nice people, and bringeth no profit. Only we ought to believe, that he is verily in heaven. For truly it standeth not with our weakness to comprehend and discern the privity of the heavens; but it beseemeth our faith to have the worthy and

[1 Sedere quoque ad dexteram Patris carnis assumtæ mysterium est; neque enim incorporeæ illi naturæ convenienter ista absque assumtione carnis aptantur; neque sedis cœlestis profectum divina natura, sed humana conquirit. Ruffini Expos. in Symbolum apud Cyprian. p. 163. ed. Fell. Oxon. 1700.]

glorious body of the Lord in high and worthy estimation[2]."
Hitherto Augustine.

CHAPTER X.

THAT CHRIST SITTETH AT THE RIGHT HAND OF GOD BY HIS HUMANITY, BUT CIRCUMSCRIBED IN PLACE, AND IS NOT EVERY WHERE.

Now, though the heavenly honour and glory be high, and may not be expressed; yet the place where he dwelleth is certain, and the body that is in heaven cannot be every where. For the right hand of God, in and after this first signification thereof, is not infinite. Else must all faithful believers also, and they that are saved, be every where, seeing they are with the Son of God, who is taken up into heaven. For the Lord himself saith: " Now from henceforth shall I be no more in the world; but they are in the world: and I come unto thee." Upon this he saith: " Father, whom thou hast given unto me, I will that where I am they also be with me, that they may see my glory which thou hast given me." Item, " He that doth me service, let him follow me: and where I am, there also shall my servants be." Seeing now that our souls, and our bodies also, after the resurrection of the flesh shall be in heaven, as in a place certain; it followeth, that the body of the Lord, which into heaven is taken up, hath also a place certain in heaven, and that the right hand of God in this signification cannot be every where. John xvii.

John xii.

In this upright matter let it trouble no man that is read in St Paul, how that " Christ ascended up above all the heavens:" by means whereof a curious body might peradventure conclude, if Christ our Lord be taken up above the heavens, then can there no place certain be ascribed unto him; seeing there is no place about or without the heaven. Ephes. iv.

[2 Sed ubi et quomodo sit in cœlo corpus Dominicum, curiosissimum et supervacaneum est quærere: tantummodo in cœlo esse credendum est. Non enim est fragilitatis nostræ cœlorum secreta discutere, sed est nostræ fidei de Dominici corporis dignitate sublimia et honesta sapere. August. De Fide et Symbolo cap. 6. Opera, Tom. III. p. 33. E. ed. 1541.]

Neither ought it to offend any man that is written, how that "unto Christ there is given a name, which is above all names;" and that Paul saith: "Neither eye hath seen, neither ear heard, nor is come into the heart of man, what God hath prepared unto them that love him." For the scripture of God throughout doth witness constantly and sure, that Jesus Christ is taken up into heaven, and sitteth at the right hand of his Father. Whereby it is out of doubt, that the Apostle thought not to set Christ without heaven; but therefore proponeth he the matter with so high and excellent words, to shew and declare unto us, that the body of our Lord, which afore was despised and shamefully defaced, is now in the supreme and brightest glory; and that meaneth he, when he saith, "above all heavens." For [whoso] doth thoroughly cons[ider the] place of Paul to the [Ephesians], findeth that Paul [doth set the] two parts of his oration, [the] one against the other. For he saith thus: "That he ascended, what meaneth it, but that he also descended first into the lowest parts of the earth?" Against this setteth he now: "He that descended, is even the same also that ascendeth up, even above all heavens." Therefore is here the one set against the other; namely, to descend into the lowest parts of the earth, and to ascend above all heavens. But who would here conclude, Christ descended into the lowest parts of the earth; ergo, he had no place upon earth? For every man understandeth well, that Paul with these words minded to declare the true coming of the Lord upon earth, and the great humility and meekness of our Lord Jesus Christ. Therefore who would then in the other part of the oration conclude, Christ ascended up above all heavens; ergo, he is not in heaven, or in any other place? For is there also any one place without the heaven? Who understandeth not now, that Paul here minded to say nothing else, than that which he uttereth more plainly to the Philippians, "He hath exalted him on high?" And though this height of heavenly honour be greater and more glorious, than any man's tongue can or may express, yet the heaven is and doth contain still the dwelling of the faithful; and therefore is it a place certain. Wherefore after my plain and simple understanding, which is not curious, I believe constantly, that the glorified body of Christ is ascended up

[Phil. ii.]
1 Cor. ii.

Phil. ii.

above all heavens, that is, above all compass, or sphere, or height of heaven; and so even in heaven, that is, in the dwelling of the faithful; and there remaineth, and is not, as they say, passed by on the outside of heaven.

For the truth witnesseth evidently: "Where I am, there shall also my servants be." Now shall the servants of God be in heaven, and not without, or above the heaven, that is to say, in no place. For Paul, the chosen man of God, saith to the Philippians: "Our dwelling is in heaven, from whence we look for the Saviour Jesus Christ." Plainly also and evidently doth the true word of God declare, that the heaven, into the which Christ ascended, is a place certain; for the Lord saith: "In my Father's house are many dwellings: if it were not so, I would have told you: I go to prepare a place for you. And if I go to prepare a place for you, I will come to you again, and receive you even unto myself; that where I am, there you may be also." John xii.
Phil. iii.
Jesus Christ.
John xiv.

There indeed could nothing be brought forth more meet and convenient to our purpose. For the thing that we now treat of is the heaven, which is the dwelling and native country of the blessed, and which here is called a dwelling, or mansion, or place; yea, a dwelling and place in the house of God the Father.

Who is now any more so malapert or arrogant, as to undertake to deny that heaven is a place? For thus saith the Lord: 'In my Father's house already there are many mansions, that not only I, but all mine also have a place and dwelling. If it were not so, then had I told you, that I would go to prepare the same for you. But now it is not needful; seeing they be prepared already, and wait for you. Whereas I now go away, and must be from you a little season, it is not that I would prepare mansions for you, for they are prepared already; but that I through my death may make the way for you into heaven, and open the street to the said dwelling.'

Now to the intent no man shall say, that we haply have a place in heaven, as men, but Christ hath not so a place; therefore doth the truth of God plainly express, that the place where Christ is is a place indeed. For he saith: "I will take you unto me;" yea, not only unto me, but unto myself: for immediately upon the same doth he yet add it more plain, "that where I am, there you may be also."

Christ then, as a very true man, is in heaven, as in one place: wherefore it followeth, that we also shall be in heaven, as in one place certain. This the Truth saith: therefore must it needs be even so, and can be none otherwise.

The same also doth the human kind and nature require; "which God," as Augustine saith, "did endue with immortality, but took not away the nature and kind[1]."

The Seleucians' error. The Seleuciani, or Hermiani, denied our Saviour Christ after the flesh to sit at the right hand of the Father[2]. But the true faithful believers have ever still confessed and taught, that the very true body or flesh of our Lord doth sit at the Father's right hand. For verily, if the body and flesh of our Lord have not his place given him, or if that be withdrawn from him, then is this the plain meaning, that our Lord had no true body.

For holy Augustine saith, and saith right: "Take all room and place from the bodies, that they have no place to be in, and they are no where; if they be no where, then are they nothing at all[3]." As for the place of Paul to the Philippians in the second chapter, it teacheth nothing at all, that with the exaltation and ascension of Christ any thing is withdrawn from the nature human, or that we ought to speak nothing more of it, or we should or might ascribe no name and place unto it; but like as with the words going before, which serve much to the matter, he thought to express the lowest humility of Christ, even so is it now his mind, with very honourable and high excellent words to set forth his glory.

[1 Carnis forma et substantia...cui profecto immortalitatem dedit, naturam non abstulit. August. Epistolæ. Ad Dardanum Epist. lvii. Opera, Tom. II. p. 56. M. See above, p. 154, note 1.]

[2 The Seleuciani and Hermiani taught that the body of Christ ascended no farther than the sun, in which it was deposited, as we are informed by Augustine: Seleuciani vel Hermiani ab auctoribus Seleuco et Hermia...negant Salvatorem in carne sedere ad dextram Patris; sed ea se exuisse perhibent, eamque in sole posuisse, accipientes occasionem de Psalmo, ubi legitur, *In sole posuit tabernaculum suum.* De Hær. Opera, Tom. VI. p. 6. I. ed. 1541. See bishop Pearson on the Creed, Art. VI., who mentions that the same heresy was held by the Manichees, and also by Hermogenes.]

[3 Nam spatia locorum tolle corporibus, nusquam erunt; et quia nusquam erunt, nec erunt. August. Epist. lvii. ad Dardanum. Opera, Tom. II. p. 57. G. ed. 1541.]

Yea, he declareth himself in the words following, and saith: "In the name of Jesus shall all knees bow, both of things that are in heaven, of things that are on the earth, and things that are under the earth." Phil. ii.

And thus hath the Father exalted the name of Jesus above all names, even in shewing and declaring that Jesus is the same, whom all they that are in heaven, upon earth, and under the earth, ought by right to know, worship, and fear, as Lord of all things and creatures; yea, and that all things should confess that Jesus is the Lord, to the praise of God the Father. For verily we must needs acknowledge that Jesus Christ is Lord, yea, Lord of all things, King, Defender, and Redeemer, of like power and honour with the Father: which thing extendeth not to the Father's derogation or dishonour, as the Arians foolishly thought, but to the greater glory of the Father. The name of Christ is above all names.
Ariani.

The Lord saith himself in the gospel: "The Father hath committed all judgment unto the Son; because that all men should honour the Son even as they honour the Father. He that honoureth not the Son, the same honoureth not the Father which hath sent him." Moreover there he saith: "And now glorify thou me, O Father, with thine own self, with the glory which I had with thee or ever the world was." From the beginning had he the honourable name of God, which is glorious and far excellent above all names. John v.

John xvii.

Now through the incarnation, and by reason of the contemned and despised cross of Christ, the godly honour in Christ was thought to be somewhat darkened. But that did the Father restore and bring to glory, in that he raised up his Son from death, and took him up into heaven. And thus gave he him a name which is above all names; for so he declared that he is Lord of all things.

Holy Peter also, a fellow-helper of St Paul, in the second chapter of the Acts of the Apostles, did in like manner utter the same. For after he hath opened and declared the true resurrection of our Lord Jesus Christ from death, and his glorious ascension into heaven, he saith: "Lo, therefore let all the house of Israel know for a surety, that God hath made this same Jesus, whom ye have crucified, Lord and Christ." And to be short, Paul by the name of Christ that is above all names understood the blessed name of Acts ii.

God the Lord, which cannot be altered, and is above all names.

But seeing our Lord is a true man, like as he is also very God, both together, and hath with the glorification not put off the kind and nature of man, neither consumed it through the Godhead; therefore remaineth he still a true creature, that is, a very true man, and therefore may he also right well be named after the same nature, and hath likewise a place certain.

<small>1 Cor. ii.</small> Finally, as for the words of the apostle Paul, "The eye hath not seen, the ear hath not heard, neither have entered into the heart of man, the things which God hath prepared for them that love him;" these matters, I say, must not be referred to the place of those that are saved. For they are written of the unoutspeakable greatness of the joy, as the whole text of the words sufficiently doth declare.

Briefly, forasmuch as it is open and manifest to us, that the Lord Jesus Christ, after his nature that he took upon him, is a very true man in glory; it followeth that the true human body of Christ hath his own place: whereof I have hitherto spoken so much not without cause, namely, to the intent all godly persons may know that this is a place certain, prepared for them in heaven, and that they may constantly believe, that in heaven they have a brother, namely, the Lord Jesus Christ. Touching the fruit of the ascension of our Lord, I shall more largely speak of it afterward.

CHAPTER XI.

ANOTHER SIGNIFICATION OF SITTING AT THE RIGHT HAND OF GOD, BY WHICH MANNER OF SITTING CHRIST IS EVERY WHERE, SITTING THERE IN SUCH SORT AFTER HIS GODHEAD.

THUS come I again to the former part, what the right hand of God signifieth and is called. It is taken in the scripture for strength, protection, power, and for the incompre-
<small>Exod. xv.</small> hensible honour or glory. And therefore it is written: "Thy right hand, Lord, is become glorious in power; thy right hand

also hath dashed the enemy." Item, in the Psalm: "Thou Psal. xviii. hast given me the defence of thy salvation; thy right hand also shall hold me up." Moreover: "The right hand of the Psal. cxviii. Lord hath the pre-eminence; the right hand of the Lord bringeth mighty things to pass." After this signification of the right hand soundeth the name, *to sit, to rule, to govern, to defend, to behave himself as a prince or regent diligently in his office, and faithfully to execute the same.* For in the third book of Kings saith David: "Solomon shall sit upon 1 Kings i. my seat, and shall reign after me." And so in the Psalm he saith: "The Lord said unto my Lord, Sit thou at my right Psal. cx. hand, till I make thine enemies thy footstool." And Paul saith: "Christ must reign, till he hath put all his enemies 1 Cor. xv. under his feet." Item, in the prophet Zachary: "Behold Zech. vi. the man, whose name is the Branch, and he that shall spring up after him shall build up the temple of the Lord; yea, even he shall build up the temple of the Lord, he shall bear the praise, he shall sit upon the Lord's throne, and have the domination; a priest shall he be also on his throne." This kind of speech is taken of the use and custom of kings and princes, which have their deputies, to whom they freely give all authority to rule and govern. Even so is Christ, in whom the Father will be honoured; and through his authority and power it is his pleasure to rule. He is taken up to the right hand of the Father, that is to say, to have the dominion or governance in heaven and in earth; and this commission is given him faithfully to execute, and to be Lord and Governor of all things.

Thus the right hand of God is infinite, neither may it be shut in; for God's might and power is incomprehensible. The kingdom of Christ also, which is everlasting, is a kingdom of all worlds; and so is he of one substance, of one power and honour, with the Father, not bound to one place, but is every where; who in all things ruleth and worketh, seeing he is not only a very true man, but also the very true God; after the manhood finite, but after his Godhead infinite and incomprehensible; and that in one undivided person he containeth very true God and man, King and Lord of all things. For St Peter saith: "Christ is at the right hand 1 Pet. iii. of God, gone up into heaven, angels, might, and power being subdued unto him." Item, Paul to the Ephesians: "God the

Father raised up Christ from the dead, and hath set him on his right hand in heavenly things, above all rule, power, might, and domination, and above all names that are named, not in this world only, but also in the world to come; and hath put all things under his feet, and hath made him above all things, and head of the congregation, which is his body, and the fulness of him that filleth all in all things." Thus much concerning the right hand of God, and concerning heaven, that is, the place certain or dwelling of the blessed; in the which also our Lord Jesus with his body hath his mansion and seat.

CHAPTER XII.

THE FRUIT AND COMMODITY OF THE CORPORAL ASCENSION OF CHRIST, BOTH IN THAT HE DOTH NOW FOR US, AND IN THAT WE LEARN BY IT.

AFTER this from henceforth will I speak of the fruit and profit of the corporal ascension of our Lord Jesus Christ, and of his seat and place at the right hand of his Father. Afore all things we must know, that our Lord ascended up with his very true body, that he, as mediator between God and man, being very God and man himself, and high priest in his own temple, might before his heavenly Father make intercession for us, and wholly take upon himself our necessities and griefs. For Paul saith to the Hebrews: "Christ is not entered into the holy places that are made with hands, which are similitudes of true things, but is entered into the new heaven, to appear now in the sight of God for us." Thereto also pertain other sentences and testimonies of John in his first epistle.

Item, of Paul to the Romans, wherein he saith: According to the same did our Lord ascend up bodily, that he with his flesh taken up into heaven might stay and direct upon the Holy Ghost all worshipping and God's service of those that are his. For no corporal worshipping doth from henceforth please him, but such as is done to his spiritual body.

He saith in the gospel of John: "The poor have ye alway with you, and when ye will, ye may do them good; but me have ye not alway." Thereunto also serveth the saying of Paul: "Although we have known Christ after the flesh, yet know we him so no more." John xii.
Mark xiv.

2 Cor. v.

Moreover the Lord with his resurrection hath taught us, that we also should lift up our minds unto heaven, seeking no salvation at all upon earth, seeing that heaven is our right native country. Therefore ought we to use the world as though we used it not, and to direct all our care and thought unto heavenly things. For Paul saith to the Colossians: "Set your affection on things which are above, and not on things which are on earth. For ye are dead, and your life is hid with Christ in God." Item, to the Philippians: "Our dwelling is in heaven, from whence we look for the Saviour, even Jesus Christ our Lord." 1 Cor. vii.

Coloss. iii.

Philip. iii.

Christ also with his ascension into heaven thought to declare unto us his power and might, wherein consisteth our strength, our power, riches, triumph against sin, death, world, devil, and hell.

For he ascending up on high led captivity captive, and when he had spoiled the enemies, he gave gifts unto his people, and endueth them yet daily with spiritual riches. Therefore sitteth he now on high, to the intent that with his own strength, which he daily bestoweth upon us, he may regenerate us unto a spiritual life, and quicken us with his holy Spirit, garnishing the church, that is to say, the faithful, with manifold gifts of thanks, defending them against all evil, suppressing the terror of his enemies, but preserving and saving us, as those that do truly honour and worship him. For he, as having the victorious triumph, is the King, Saviour, and head of all faithful believers. Ephes. iv.

Finally, also with his resurrection he hath prepared us a place, and made the way and opened it into heaven. Thus in heaven hath he placed the true man, that we might have an assured true testimony, that our flesh also shall rise again, and that the whole perfect man, the body and soul, shall be carried into heaven. For the members shall be like unto the head. Therefore as the cloud took up the very true body of the Lord, yea, even the whole perfect man, Christ; so shall all godly persons be taken up into the air to meet the Lord, that they may live in Christ their Lord and head for evermore. For Paul saith: "The dead in Christ shall arise first. Then we which live and remain shall be caught up with them also in the clouds, to meet the Lord in the air, and so shall we ever be with the Lord." Item, to the Hebrews: "By the means of the blood of Jesu we have free entrance into the holy place, by the new and living way, which he hath prepared for us through the veil, that is to say, by his flesh." Unto this meaning agreeth very well the godly and excellent sentence of the old writer Tertullian, who in the book of *The resurrection of the flesh* saith thus: "Christ, which is called the arbiter and mediator between God and man, hath of the same that is set and committed unto him of both, reserved also unto himself the adding to of the flesh, for an earnest-penny of the whole sum. For like as he hath left us the pledge of the Spirit, even so contrariwise hath he received of us the earnest-penny of the flesh, and carried it up with him into heaven; a true evidence or pledge, that he will bring thither also the whole sum, body and soul[1]." For this great and high benefit, declared unto us by his own mercy without our deserving, be laud and praise, honour and thanks unto our King, our victorious triumpher, head, and Redeemer, even our Lord Jesus Christ, from henceforth, now, for evermore. Amen.

[1 Hic sequester Dei atque hominum appellatus, ex utriusque partis commisso deposito sibi, carnis quoque depositum servat in semetipso, arrhabonem summæ totius. Quemadmodum enim nobis arrhabonem Spiritus reliquit, ita et a nobis arrhabonem carnis accepit, et vexit in cœlum, pignus totius summæ illuc quandoque redigendæ. Tertull. De Resurr. Carn. cap. 51, p. 357. Ed. Rigalt. 1564.]

THE

SECOND PART OF THIS BOOK,

ENTITLED

THE HOPE OF THE FAITHFUL,

ENTREATING OF OUR BODIES.

CHAPTER XIII.

OF THE TRUE RESURRECTION OF OUR FLESH.

Now cometh it to the point, that we must also speak of the true raising up of our bodies, or resurrection of this our flesh; for the same followeth out of the resurrection and ascension of our Lord Jesus Christ. This word, *to rise up*, as Tertullian *De resurrectione carnis* declareth, extendeth to nothing more, than unto that which was fallen[2]. For nothing can arise, save only it that fell. For when a thing was fallen and standeth up again, we say, it is risen. Forasmuch as this term, *to rise up*, hath a relation, St Paul useth the word *Anistemi* (ἀνίστημι), which signifieth *to erect, to rise up, to set up again*, and *to stand*. *Egeiromai ex hypnou* (Ἐγείρομαι ἐξ ὕπνου), *I arise up and awake from sleep*. The Hebrews use the word *Kum* (קום), which signifieth not only *to rise up*, but also *to endure, to continue*, and *to remain upright*. For in the book of Joshua we read: "The children Josh. vii. of Israel could not stand before their enemies," that is, they might not endure and continue before them. Furthermore, in the book of Genesis: "Every thing was destroyed, that Gen. vii. remained (that is, whatsoever there was that stood upright, or erected itself) upon the face of the earth." Thereof it cometh, that to stand up, and to raise up, is called the immortality, or the everlasting and perpetual continuance of the

[2 De Resurr. Carn. cap. 18, p. 336; also Adv. Marcion. Lib. v. cap. 9, p. 471.]

John vi. soul. As when the Lord saith in the Gospel of John: "I will raise him up at the last day." For if by the last day the hour of every man's death be understood, then doth the Lord raise up, that is, he preserveth, the soul in the state that it dieth not, neither perisheth in death. Now if by the last day be understood doomsday, then raiseth he up the body from the earth at the last day in the general judgment. Therefore the words, *to stand up, and rise up*, signify either the conservation of a thing which is, that it be not destroyed and perish, or else the restoring of a thing that was fallen to his right case and estate again.

CHAPTER XIV.

OUR FLESH OR BODY ITSELF SHALL RISE AGAIN, THOUGH IT BE HARD TO BELIEVE, AND WHAT THE FLESH OR BODY IS.

Now will we speak also of these terms, flesh and body, or corpse. We believe the resurrection of the body or flesh.

The scripture commonly calleth it the resurrection of the dead, to declare evidently, that the resurrection must not be referred to the soul nor to the spirit, but directly unto the body and to the flesh. Cyprianus, or Ruffinus, saith, that the church towards the west did express and acknowledge the article in the holy apostolical creed after this manner: "I believe the resurrection of the flesh:" and so they added thereunto manifestly this term, *the*, to the intent that no man should understand any other flesh, save only the same natural and essential flesh which we carry about[1]." So saith Augustine

[1 Satis provida et cauta adjectione fidem symboli ecclesia nostra docet, quæ in eo quod a' ceteris traditur, *carnis resurrectionem*, uno addito pronomine tradit, *hujus carnis resurrectionem; hujus* sine dubio, quam is, qui profertur, signaculo crucis fronti imposito contingit; quo sciat unusquisque fidelium, carnem suam, si mundam servaverit a peccato, futuram esse vas honoris, utile Domino, ad omne opus bonum paratum; si vero contaminata fuerit in peccatis, futuram esse vas iræ ad interitum. Ruffin. Expos. in Symbol. Apostol. apud Cyprian. Edit. Fell.]

also in the book of the articles of the creed: "The same visible, which properly is called flesh, shall without doubt and assuredly rise up again[2]."

Methinketh that Paul the apostle minded to point unto the flesh, as with a finger; and therefore said: "This corruptible must put on incorruption." With the term, *this*, pointeth he, as with a finger, to our flesh.

_{1 Cor. xv.}

Holy Jerome forceth and compelleth John, the bishop of Jerusalem, to confess and acknowledge the resurrection, not only of the body, but also of the flesh, and saith: "The flesh and the body are two things. Every flesh is a body, but every body is not flesh; namely, a wall is a body, but flesh it is not. For flesh is properly called a substance of blood, sinews, bones, and veins set together. As for a body, though the name thereof also be used for flesh, and most part for a substance that may be seen or handled; yet it betokeneth sometimes a subtle state, that can neither be handled nor seen, as namely the air[3]." But at all times it hath been a hard thing for man to believe, that bodies which are buried and resolved to corruption, should wholly, without imperfection or blemish, be brought again and restored. Therefore the Athenians, when they heard of the holy apostle the resurrection of the dead, they mocked and laughed his doctrine to scorn. For who would lightly credit, that the bodies which now are corrupt and returned to earth, or otherwise torn and devoured of wild beasts and fowls, yea, sometimes burnt and brought to ashes, or drowned with water, should perfectly be brought again, and wholly restored?

_{What the body or corpse is called of the Latinists.}

[2 Et ideo credimus et carnis resurrectionem, non tantum quia reparatur anima, quæ nunc propter carnales affectiones caro nostra nominatur; sed etiam hæc visibilis caro, quæ naturaliter est caro, cujus nomen anima non propter naturam, sed propter affectiones carnales accepit. Hæc ergo visibilis, quæ proprie caro dicitur, sine dubitatione credenda est resurgere. August. de Fid. et Symb. cap. 10. Opera, Tom. III. p. 34. G. Ed. 1541.]

[3 Alia carnis, alia corporis definitio est: omnis enim caro corpus est, non omne corpus est caro. Caro est proprie, quæ sanguine, venis, ossibus, nervisque constringitur. Corpus, quanquam et caro dicatur, interdum tamen ætherium aut aereum nominatur, quod tactui visuique subjacet, et plerumque visibile est et tangibile. Hieron. Epist. XXXVIII. ad Pammach. adversus errores Joannis Hierosolymitani. Opera, Tom. IV. p. 322. Ed. 1706.]

But God, willing to make that easy and light, which is hard unto us, hath in the resurrection of our Lord Jesus Christ set before our eyes an open, plain, and sure trial, declaration, or evidence of the true undoubted resurrection: whereunto, as to an ensample and sure strength of the resurrection, we ought to have respect, as much and as oft as we think upon it, and wonder how our bodies should rise again.

Therefore with so many testimonies and arguments have I declared afore, that Christ our Lord with his own body rose truly again from death. He carried up Elias also living, body and soul, into heaven, and many one raised he up from the dead; that we, concerning the resurrection of the dead, should have utterly no doubt at all. Finally, with plain and evident testimonies of the scripture hath he opened and shewed, as I now will declare: which testimonies and arguments truly do teach, that the flesh of men shall rise again from the dead, that is, that our bodies shall at the last day be truly raised up unto judgment. Holy Job saith thus in chapter xix.: "O that my words now were written! O that they were put into a book! would God they were graven with an iron pen in lead or in stone to continue! For I am sure that my Redeemer liveth; and that he shall stand over the dust, or earth, in the latter day; that I shall be clothed again with this skin, and see God in my flesh. Yea, I myself, or for myself, shall behold him, not another, but with these same eyes. My reins are consumed within me." Job's adversaries complained of him, as though he knew not God, and as though he set nothing by him. Upon this great slander and blasphemy, he answereth and declareth his faith, desiring that his belief were written in lead and in hard stone, that is, he wisheth his faith to be known to those that come after, which he also declareth with few words after this manner: 'I am of you complained upon and accused, as though I knew not God; now do I know right well in my heart, yea, I believe and am certified assuredly, that my Redeemer, or Avenger, liveth.' The holy Job useth an Hebrew word called *Goel*[1], which some have expounded a *Redeemer*: it signifieth a *rescuer*, and an *avenger;* such one as is more friend of ours, such as were they, to whom in the law of the Jews

[1 גֹּאֵל]

it appertained to redeem the goods, and to rescue them; as we may learn further out of Ruth, and of the fourth book of Moses: and with the aforesaid name, *Goel*, hath Job set forth and specified the Messias, our Lord Jesus Christ; that he liveth, namely, that he is the true living God, the life and resurrection of men; and that he is also the rescuer and avenger, doubtless even the same that is our very near friend; namely, a very true man, such one as hath taken our own flesh and blood upon him, suffered death, and with his death hath made us living. Moreover he saith: "At the last shall he stand over the dust." For our Lord Jesus Christ, with his very true body, shall come at the last day to judge, and then shall he stand over the dust. This saying declareth evidently, that he will undertake and do somewhat, namely, that he shall put to his mighty hand, so order and bring to pass, that the dust shall come to life again. The dust calleth he here our flesh, and that according to the scripture; and with this doth he wonderful well express the truth of our flesh, namely, that our own very true flesh shall rise again. For he will certify us, that even the very same body, which at the first was made of dust, and now into dust is sown, and through the corruption is become dust again, yea, even that same very body, and none other, shall be raised up. ^{Ruth iv.} ^{Num. xxxv.} ^{Gen. iii.}

But to the intent that no man should draw or refer the dust to any other thing, than to the body of man, it followeth moreover in holy Job, that after they, namely, the Father, the Son, and the Holy Ghost, have with my skin (not with a strange, but with mine own skin) clothed the body, even mine own body which I now have, called dust, (and thereby understandeth he the flesh, the sinews and the bones;) then shall I see God in my flesh, that is, fully and perfectly shall I be restored and made whole again. For to see God is nothing else but to be partaker of eternal joy and salvation; and to see God in or from out of the flesh, is to be taken up corporally into everlasting joy. Besides this, he doth yet more evidently express the perfectness of the resurrection of the flesh, and saith: "Whom I for myself shall see," that is, to my commodity and salvation, mine eyes shall see him, even I myself shall see him, and none other for me. In the which words it is principally to be noted, that he saith, "I shall see him," yea, even I myself. Then, "mine eyes shall see him." Finally, "I, and else none other." As he would say, 'Even I that now have true flesh and bone, and look now upon you with mine eyes, shall with the very same eyes behold God also.' Therefore in the resurrection of the dead we shall with the essential substance and nature be even the same that we were before death, namely, we shall have our members, as head, eyes, bones, belly, arms, legs, hands, feet, &c. Now where this distinction is, there must be also circumscription, there must the same have compass and limits.

It followeth yet further in Job: "My reins," namely, my desire and lust, "are wasted away, and consumed within me," that is, within me, namely, in my heart, or ceased all other desires, lusts, and pleasures, in comparison of this my hope towards the resurrection; yea, in comparison thereof they all are nothing, neither worthy to be esteemed: for in the only resurrection resteth all my hope and delight. So said Paul also: "I have counted all things but loss, and do judge them but dung, that I might win Christ, to know him and the virtue of his resurrection." And therefore the old translator of the book of Job hath evil interpreted these words after the sense, "this hope is laid up in my heart[1]."

Phil. iii.

After all this, doth holy Job add hereunto that maketh the understanding perfect, and concludeth his saying thus: "Seeing I thus acknowledge and confess, why hold ye me for ungodly? Why do ye persecute and vex me thus with spiteful words of reproach and slander? Yet is the root of the word found in me." And he calleth the root of the word the right foundation and ground of godliness: as if he would say: "Forasmuch as the true head article of salvation is found in me." For like as the root giveth all virtue and sap unto the tree, even so is the matter of the resurrection of the dead through Christ the chiefest, greatest, and true principal point of the word and affairs of God. "Repent therefore," saith Job: "for wrath humbleth, and

[1 The original is: כָּלוּ כִלְיֹתַי בְּחֵקִי ; of which the meaning is expressed in the Latin Vulgate by, *reposita est hæc spes in sinu meo;* adopting, as Rosenmuller has observed, a meaning of the word כָּלָה, which is found in different passages, "*de vehementissimo desiderio, quo quis consumitur quasi et deficit.*" Comp. Psalm lxxxiv. 3, cxix. 81, 82, 123, cxliii. 7.]

doth nothing right, but rather provoketh God unto vengeance."

The prophet Isaiah doth testify the resurrection after this manner: "Thy dead shall live, even with my body shall they arise. Stand up and be glad, ye that rest, or dwell, in the dust; for the dew of the herbs is thy dew, and the ground of tyrants shalt thou cast down." "Thy dead, O God," saith the prophet, "shall live;" namely, the souls that for thy sake are slain, and that have worshipped thee. Nevertheless their bodies shall not prevent my body in the resurrection; but at the last judgment, or upon doomsday, shall they arise again with my body. Likewise saith also St Peter, that the souls of such as died aforetime do live with God; but with the flesh they shall be judged as other men. Isai. xxvi. 1 Pet. iv.

Therefore did the holy prophet Isaiah believe and confess the general resurrection of all bodies at the last day. In the which resurrection, he openly acknowledgeth, that his own body also shall rise again. Afterward bringeth he in an archangel, blowing the trumpet, and saying: "Stand up, and be glad, ye that rest in the dust." To rest in dust is nothing else but a description of man's body. For the souls and spirits do not rest or lie in dust; but the bodies are buried therein, and are become dust. Therefore men, according to the substance and state thereof wherein they rise again, are called inhabiters, or indwellers of dust, or such as rest in dust. Then declareth he with a similitude, how our bodies, that putrefy and corrupt, shall, through the power of God, from death and corruption be safely raised up again. To rest in dust.

The power of God, that chargeth and commandeth us to rise up from death, doth he compare to the dew, which, when it falleth down, quickeneth and reviveth the dead herbs. Likewise also doth the power of God to our dead bodies, which it quickeneth and raiseth up again. Contrary to this he setteth another sentence, saying: "The earth of tyrants, that is, the bodies of tyrants, shalt thou raise up, O God; but thou shalt cast them down," that is, thou shalt overthrow them into hell and eternal pain. Moreover, touching the true resurrection of our bodies, the vision of the prophet Ezekiel is so evident and plain, that it is not needful to speak aught thereof. Ezek. xxxvii.

And of this have we many testimonies and witnesses in the prophets, which might here well have served; but seeing it is not necessary, I have because of shortness omitted them, and now will I come to the sentences of the new Testament.

<small>John v.</small> The Lord saith: "Verily, verily, I say unto you, the hour shall come, and now it is, that the dead shall hear the voice of the Son of God, and they that hear it shall live." And immediately after he saith: "The hour shall come, in the which all they that are in the graves shall hear his voice, and shall come forth." Now is it manifest, that neither the souls, nor spirits, but the bodies are in the graves; and if other bodies should rise up for ours, what needed he alway to make mention of the graves, but to the intent that he immediately in the gospel might declare the evident, plain, and undoubted resurrection of our bodies? He forthwith, by <small>John xi.</small> his mighty and wonderful power, raised up Lazarus from death, who now did stink, and had lain four days in the grave. This marvellous act had the Lord himself declared unto Martha with these words: "Thy brother shall rise again. Then answered she, I know that he shall rise in the resurrection at the last day." Lo, how common, manifest, and known unto every man was the general resurrection of our bodies. The Lord saith more unto Martha: "I am the resurrection and the life: he that believeth on me, though he were dead, yet shall he live; and every one that liveth and believeth on me, shall never die." But what needeth me to collect so many testimonies of the resurrection of the dead, considering that the apostles were upon no article more fervent and earnest than upon this? He that will allege all the sentences and witnesses, must write out almost the whole new Testament. <small>Acts iv.</small> Luke saith in the Acts of the Apostles: "With great power did the apostles bear witness of the resurrection of the Lord <small>Acts xxiii.</small> Jesus Christ." And in the same book saith Paul: "For the hope and resurrection of the dead am I judged." And <small>Acts xxviii.</small> yet again: "For the hope sake of Israel am I bound with this chain." In many places hath the holy apostle Paul brought forth evident ensamples and testimonies of our resurrection; concerning the which we shall speak in due time. <small>2 Cor. iv.</small> He saith moreover: "We which live are always delivered unto death for Jesus' sake, that the life of Jesus might ap-

pear in our mortal bodies." What could he have spoken more evident and plain? For immediately upon the same he saith: "Thus we have believed: therefore have we spoken; and know, that he which raised up the Lord Jesus, shall through Jesus raise us up also." Wherefore our true bodies, which now are mortal, shall verily rise again; howbeit after the resurrection they shall no more be mortal, but immortal.

To these witnesses out of God's word, and therefore invincible, I will also add the testimony of one man, namely, out of the fourth book of John Damascen *De orthodoxa fide*, Cap. 28. "The resurrection," saith he, "shall be nothing else but a true conjunction of soul and body, and another laudable restitution of it that was fallen away, and brought to nought. Therefore the same body that perisheth is dissolved and fallen asunder, and the very same riseth up again indissoluble. For he that in the beginning created man out of the dust of the earth, and then brought him again to earth and dust, that he was taken of, the same, I say, is mighty and of power, according to his word, to raise up the selfsame man again from death[1]." Thus much Damascenus. And truly every man now may well think, that God principally for this cause did not create the first man of nought, as he did other things, but out of the dust of the earth; that as concerning the resurrection of our bodies, though they turn to dust and earth again, we should have no doubt. Now, as I suppose, I have sufficiently and plainly declared, that the true flesh of all men, yea, even our own body, and else none for it, yea, even the human true body shall rise again from death, namely, formed and fashioned with his own right proportion, measure, and property, as a true body; so that the measure and property of the true body, which now is divided and parted in his members and joints, remaineth, that is, he shall have true flesh, blood, bones, sinews, joints, members, &c.

_{Johannes Damascenus.}

[1 Ἀνάστασίς ἐστι πάντως, συνάφεια πάλιν ψυχῆς τε καὶ σώματος, καὶ δευτέρα τοῦ διαλυθέντος καὶ πεσόντος ζώου στάσις. αὐτὸ οὖν τὸ σῶμα τὸ φθειρόμενον καὶ διαλυόμενον, αὐτὸ ἀναστήσεται ἄφθαρτον· οὐκ ἀδυνατεῖ γὰρ ὁ ἐν ἀρχῇ ἐκ τοῦ χοὸς τῆς γῆς αὐτὸ συστησάμενος, πάλιν ἀναλυθὲν καὶ ἀποστραφὲν εἰς τὴν γῆν, ἐξ ἧς ἐλήφθη, κατὰ τὴν τοῦ δημιουργοῦ ἀπόφασιν, πάλιν ἀναστῆσαι αὐτό. Joann. Damasc. De Orthod. Fide, Lib. IV. cap. 27. Opera, Tom. I. p. 321. Ed. 1712.]

CHAPTER XV.

THE MANNER HOW THE BODIES SHALL RISE AGAIN, AND THE KIND THAT THEY SHALL BE OF.

But to the intent that this may yet be more plainly understood, I will now tell how our bodies shall rise, and what nature and kind they shall be of in the resurrection. At the end of the world shall the Lord come with great majesty and judgment, and shall declare and shew himself in and with a right true essential body. Hither also too shall he be brought, and shall stand in the clouds of heaven, that all flesh may see him; yea, all men that are upon earth shall behold him, and know him by his glory. In the mean season also shall he send his archangel to blow the trump. Then shall all the dead hear, and perceive the voice and power of the Son of God. And so all men that died, from the first Adam, shall immediately arise out of the earth.

And all they that live until the last day shall, in the twinkling of an eye, be changed. And thus all men, every one in his own flesh, shall stand before the judgment-seat of our Lord Jesus Christ, and shall wait for the last judgment and sentence of the Lord; which sentence being given, quickly, and without delay, (he) shall call one part into heaven, and thrust out the other into hell.

This fashion and manner of the resurrection have not I imagined of myself, but written it all out of the evangelists and scriptures of the holy apostles. For thus we read: " The power of heaven shall move in the last time, and then shall appear the sign of the Son of man in heaven; and then shall all the kindreds of the earth mourn, and they shall see the Son of man come in the clouds of heaven with power and great glory. And he shall send his angels with the great voice of a trumpet, and they shall gather together his chosen from the four winds, and from the one end of the world to the other," &c. Thereunto add that he spake in Matthew and John. And Paul in the first to the Thessalonians saith: " This say we unto you in the word of the Lord; that we which live and are remaining in the coming of the Lord,

<small>Matth. xxiv.</small>

<small>Matth. xxv. John v.</small>

<small>1 Thess. iv.</small>

shall not come before them which sleep. For the Lord himself shall descend from heaven with a shout, and the voice of the archangel, and trump of God: and the dead in Christ shall rise first. Then shall we that live and remain be caught up with them also in the clouds, to meet the Lord in the air; and so shall we ever be with the Lord." Furthermore to the Corinthians saith Paul: "Behold, I shew you a mystery: we shall not all sleep, but we shall all be changed, and that in a moment, in the twinkling of an eye, at the time of the last trump. For the trump shall blow, and the dead shall rise incorruptible, and we shall be changed. For this corruptible must put on incorruption, and this mortal must put on immortality." This is now the manner of the resurrection of our bodies, and in what nature and kind they shall rise again. But in the resurrection they shall, through the power of God, be made immortal and incorruptible. For the apostle saith expressly: "The dead shall rise again." After that he saith: "This corruptible and mortal must put on incorruption and immortality." In the which words the term "*this*" pointeth directly, as with a finger, to our living and human body. _{1 Cor. xv.}

And so Job said: "Even I myself shall see him, and none other." Wherefore our bodies, after they be risen again from death, shall remain even in their own right state and substance, as afore. Yea, even the very same men shall keep still this nature and kind, as they did afore; saving that they which aforetime were subject to frailty shall from thenceforth be pure, clean, perfect, immortal, of a sincere and purified nature, subject and obedient unto the spirit. _{Job xix.}

Such bodies raised from death did the old writers call glorified, purified, or glorious bodies; and that according to the doctrine of the holy apostles. Albeit there were some which abused that word, and therefore made the verity of the bodies void and of none effect, beginning to dispute of glorified bodies, as of the pure substance and estate of a spirit. Whereof we shall speak shortly, if God will. _{What a glorified body is.}

CHAPTER XVI.

THAT PAUL SPAKE RIGHTLY OF A GLORIFIED BODY, AND WHAT A GLORIFIED BODY IS, AND WHAT A NATURAL.

<small>Phil. iii.</small>

BUT now will I declare, that Paul did rightly and well use this word glorious, or glorified body, even as it is truly in itself. For to the Philippians he saith: " Our dwelling is in heaven: from whence we look for the Saviour, even Jesus Christ the Lord; which shall change our vile earthy body, that it may be fashioned like unto his own glorious body, according to the working whereby he is able to subdue all things unto himself." In this sentence thou hast that term, *glorified body;* thou hast also of what nature and kind the glorified body shall be, namely, whole, and as the body of Christ that rose again from death. And thus shall it not be a body utterly made void or brought to nothing, or altogether turned into a spirit, and therefore having no room and place, incomprehensible and invisible; but it shall be an upright, very true human body, as it is sufficiently declared afore, where I spake of the true resurrection of the Lord. In the which place we understand, that when the Lord's disciples thought they had seen a spirit, when they saw the Lord,

<small>Luke xxiv.</small>

he said unto them: "A spirit hath not flesh and bones, as ye see me have. Handle me and see; for it is even I myself." The Lord also after his resurrection set before them some fashion or evidence of his glorification, namely, when he was transfigured before them; and at the time remained the right essential substance of the body; but in form and fashion it was altered, in that it became glorious. So standeth it plainly, "he was transfigured," and not that he was made void or brought to nothing, or altered into another substance.

<small>Phil. iii.</small>

Thus saith Paul also: "He shall change our body," &c. Wherefore even the right true substance of the glorified body shall remain still. As for the change or alteration, it shall be in the infirmities that happen unto us; so that when the body taketh upon it the glorification and immortality, they shall be wholly removed and fall away.

Howbeit this shall be more evident and plain to understand, if it be thoroughly and with diligence considered and declared, what this word *glory* or *glorification* meaneth.

For transfiguration, glory, and glorification, is one thing. So saith holy Augustine[1] in his book against the Arians: "To bring to glory, to make glorious, and to glorify, are three words, yet is it but one thing. The Greeks call it δοξάζειν, *doxazein*; but the translators in Latin have otherwise interpreted it." Thus much saith Augustine. But glory in scripture is taken for light, brightness, and shine, as St Paul speaketh to the Corinthians: "If the ministration that through the letter killeth, and was graven in stone, hath glory, so that the children of Israel could not behold the face of Moses for the glory of his countenance," &c. And hereunto serveth this sentence of Daniel the wise: "Such as have taught others shall shine as the brightness of heaven, and they that have instructed multitudes, or many, unto godliness, shall be as the stars world without end." Much after the same wise doth the Lord himself also use it, saying: "Then shall the righteous shine as the sun in the kingdom of their Father." _{Contra Aria. cap. 31.} _{2 Cor. iii.} _{Dan. xii.} _{Matth. xiii.}

Wherefore the glorified bodies shall be clear, bright, and shining bodies, even as the body of Christ was in his transfiguration upon the mount of Thabor; of whom it is specified in the gospel, that "his face was as bright as the sun, and his clothes did shine as the light." After the resurrection did the Lord shew unto his disciples his palpable and visible, that is, his very true substantial body: but the brightness and shine he reserved, to teach and instruct the weak here beneath. Like as also after the resurrection he did eat and drink, not that he needed any such thing, but that he so would declare and prove the true resurrection of his body. The glorification also is set directly against the low estate and dishonour, as Paul evidently declareth, saying: "He shall change our vile body, that he may make it like unto his own glorious and glorified body." This word *humility, low estate,* or *dishonour,* comprehendeth all that is called _{Matth. xvii.}

[[1] Glorificare, et honorificare, et clarificare, tria quidem verba, sed res una est, quod Græce dicitur δοξάζειν: interpretum autem varietate, aliter atque aliter positum est in Latino. August. Contr. Serm. Arian. cap. 31. Opera, Tom. vi. p. 146, E. Ed. 1541.]

earthy, frail, miserable, and mortal. For by means of our sins we are brought low and into misery; so that we must needs feel and suffer sickness, hunger, thirst, cold, heat, pain, vexation, manifold lusts and affections, fear, wrath, heaviness, and such like things innumerable, yea, and death also at the last.

Again, glorification comprehendeth deliverance, that is, the laying away and clear discharge of all these miseries and sorrows. So that now glorification is called (and so it is in very deed) pureness, perfect strength, immortality, and joy; yea, a sure, quiet, and everlasting life. For Paul saith: "We that are in this tabernacle sigh and are grieved; because we would not be unclothed, but we would be clothed upon, that mortality might be swallowed up of life." And to the Romans he saith thus: "I suppose that the afflictions of this life are not worthy of the glory which shall be shewed upon us. For the fervent desire of the creature abideth waiting for the appearing of the children of God."

In all these words it is sufficiently declared, what glorification meaneth, and what is understood by it; namely, a freedom or discharge from this frail servitude and bondage, and a deliverance into the glorious and comfortable liberty of God's children. By the which freedom we are delivered from all sickness and frailty, and from all thraldom of weakness, that is, from all that which bringeth sickness, heaviness, and frailty. From all such are we free discharged and delivered, having now the perfect fruition of God, and made of like shape unto his Son Jesus Christ, as holy St John declareth. Hereunto serveth it well that Paul saith: "When this corruptible hath put on incorruption, and this mortal hath put on immortality, then shall be brought to pass the saying that is written, Death is swallowed up in the victory."

Therefore the glorified body, after the signification of glory, shall be a purified body, which is purged and cleansed from all frailty and vileness, and now is clothed upon and apparelled with cleanness, pureness, joy, and rest, and finally, with the glory of eternal life. That this is now the kind and nature of the glorified body, the holy apostle Paul more largely and more perfectly declareth with these words: "It is sown in corruption, and riseth in incorruption; it is sown in dishonour, and riseth in glory; it is sown in weakness, and riseth in power; it is sown a natural body, and riseth a spiritual body." Item, what he meaneth by the natural and by the spiritual body, he declareth immediately upon the same, and saith further: "If there be a natural body, there is also a spiritual body, as it is written: The first man Adam is made into a natural life, and the last man Adam into a spiritual life. Yet is not the spiritual body the first, but the natural; and afterward the spiritual. The first man is of the earth earthy, the second man is the Lord from heaven. As is the earthy, such are they that are earthy; and as is the heavenly, such are they that be heavenly. And as we have borne the image of the earthy, so shall we bear also the image of the heavenly." This the holy apostle declareth yet more evidently, and saith: "By one man came death, and by one man cometh the resurrection of the dead. For like as in Adam they all die, so in Christ shall they all revive." Thus Paul calleth *animale corpus* the soulish body, which is interpreted, *the natural body*, the same that hath his virtue, strength, power, and life of the soul; which body we have of Adam; and it is earthy, frail, and mortal. The spiritual body he calleth not it that is become or made a spirit: but therefore nameth he the glorified body a spiritual body, because it liveth of the Spirit of Christ; which spiritual body, that is, incorruptible, indissoluble, and immortal, we have received of Christ our Lord. Of all this is sufficiently spoken in our expositions of the epistles of St Paul[1].

A natural and spiritua. body.

1 Cor. xv.

Animale et spirituale corpus.

CHAPTER XVII.

THE CASE OF OUR MEMBERS IN THE BODY'S RESURRECTION, AND OF THEIR FUNCTIONS.

But here might some man say: If our very true bodies, with their members, shall be in heaven, then it follows, that the use and exercise of the members shall be in heaven also.

[1 The author alludes to the translation of Erasmus's paraphrase of the epistles of St Paul, part of which was made by Bishop Coverdale.]

To this I give like answer as now is said, namely, that we shall have even those members and this body, which we now carry; but seeing that through the glorification they shall be made heavenly, they shall not need earthy exercise, neither shall they use any frail thing at all. Hereof cometh it that Paul saith: "Flesh and blood may not possess the kingdom of God, neither may corruption inherit incorruption." By flesh and blood he meaneth, not the true essential body, but bodily frail lusts and temptations, which he now calleth the earthy and frail body. Such temptations and lusts, saith he, shall not be in the glorified bodies, neither shall there any frail bodies be in heaven. For he saith immediately upon the same: "Corruption shall not inherit incorruption;" for in the kingdom of God there shall be no corruption nor frailty. For the heavenly joy is far of another kind and nature, than that it can receive or suffer such vile and unclean lusts and temptations, yea, such a stained and defiled flesh. For before the bodies of men come in heaven, they must be wholly and perfectly altered, that is, cleansed and purified from all filthiness and frailty.

_{1 Cor. xv.}

Thus did our Saviour teach also, when he answered to the question of the Sadducees, who denied the resurrection of the dead. Upon which I have written much in the gospel of Matthew. Holy Augustine saith also: "This doth sore hinder the ethnics and heretics, that we believe that the earthy body is taken up into heaven; for they think, that into heaven can come no earthy thing. But they know not our scripture, neither understand how it is spoken of Paul: 'It is sown a natural body, and shall rise a spiritual body.' For this is not spoken, to the intent as though the body should become a spirit, or be changed into a spirit. For even now also our body, which is called natural, or soulish, and is natural indeed, is not changed into the soul, and become the soul. But therefore is the body called a spiritual body, that it may so be prepared to dwell in heaven. Which thing cometh to pass, when all feebleness and earthy blemish is changed into a heavenly pureness and stedfastness[1]." All these are the words of holy Augustine.

_{Matth. xxii.}

_{Augustine, de fide et symbolo, cap. 6.}

[1 Solet autem quosdam offendere vel impios gentiles vel hæreticos, quod credamus assumptum terrenum corpus in cœlum. At gentiles plerumque philosophorum argumentis nobiscum agere solent,

CHAPTER XVIII.

THE DIVERS ERRORS THAT SPRUNG ABOUT THE ARTICLE OF THE BODY'S RESURRECTION.

HITHERTO have I told what the scripture of the prophets and apostles doth hold and testify concerning the resurrection of the dead, and of our body, that is to say, of our own true flesh; namely, that our true flesh and body shall rise from death, and be glorified in the resurrection; and that the glorification doth not therefore take away the verity of the body, or make it nothing, but doth translate and bring it into a more upright and better state; so that nevertheless the true essential substance of the body remaineth still. Upon this now, to the commodity of the reader, and for a more evident declaration and understanding of the aforesaid words, I will shew what errors sprung up concerning the resurrection of the dead; that any good faithful Christian may the better avoid the same. That there have been many which denied the resurrection of our bodies, and had it utterly in derision, all histories declare. In the which register the philosophers for the most part are reckoned and esteemed; the Hymeneus and Philetus, of whom Paul maketh mention. In like manner are there many recited of Irenæus, Tertullian, Eusebius, Epiphanius, Philastrius, and Augustine; namely these, the Simonians[2], Valentinians[3], Marcionites[4],

Errors touching the resurrection of the flesh.

Philosoph.

2 Tim. ii.

ut dicant, terrenum aliquid in cœlo esse non posse: nostras enim scripturas non noverunt, nec sciunt quomodo dictum sit, Seminatur corpus animale, surget corpus spiritale. Non enim dictum est, quasi corpus vertatur in spiritum et spiritus fiat: quia et nunc corpus nostrum, quod animale dicitur, non in animam versum est et anima factum. Sed spiritale corpus intelligitur, quia ita coaptandum est, ut cœlesti habitationi conveniat, omni fragilitate ac labe terrena in cœlestem puritatem et stabilitatem mutata ac conversa. August. de Fid. et Symb. cap. 6. Opera, Vol. III. p. 33. E. Ed. 1541.]

[2 Simonians. August. De Hæres. Opera, Tom. VI. p. 3. K.]

[3 Valentinians. Id. Ibid. p. 4. C. Tertull. De Præscript. Hæret. cap. 33.]

[4 Marcionites. Tertull. De Præscript. Hæret. Ib.]

Cerdonians[1], Carpocratians[2], Caines[3], Archontici[4], Generians[5], Hierarchics[6], Seleucians[7], Apellysts[8], and Manichees[9]. Among the Greeks also and Latinists there were excellent men, that turned themselves to the golden and yet earthy Jerusalem, promising much, I know not what, of a kingdom of the world to come after the resurrection, ascribing unto us such bodies as, being partakers of the kingdom, should also behold with these earthy desires[10]. To these there is found yet the third part, which as touching the substance and state of the glorified bodies so said and taught, that they utterly took away and overthrew the bodily nature, and gave unto it no more nor other thing than a spirit. Against the second sort speaketh holy Jerome, that forasmuch as they were carnal, they have also loved only the flesh. Against the third speaketh the said Jerome, that they, being unthankful for the benefits of God, would not have and bear the flesh, wherein Christ yet was born and rose again. Whereupon he giveth very godly counsel, that we tarry in the mean

[1 Cerdonians. Tertull. De Præscript. Hæret. cap. 51. August. De Hæres. Opera, Tom. VI. p. 4. F.]

[2 Carpocratians. Tertull. De Præscript. Hæret. cap. 48. August. De Hæres. Ib. p. 4. B.]

[3 Caines. August. De Hæres. Ib. p. 4. E.]

[4 Archontici. Id. Ibid. p. 4. F.]

[5 Generians. The nature of their opinions does not appear.]

[6 Hierarchics. August. De Hæres. Ib. p. 6. C.]

[7 Seleucians. Id. Ibid. p. 6. I.]

[8 Apellysts. Tertull. De Præscript. Hæret. cap. 33.]

[9 Manichees. August. Contr. Faustum Manich. Lib. IV. cap. 2. Lib. V. cap. 10. Opera, Tom. VI.]

[10 Cerinthus appears to have been the leader and chief of the persons, who held these opinions concerning the earthly Jerusalem, as we learn from the fragments of Caius, (Euseb. Hist. Eccles. Lib. III. cap. 28, and Caii Fragmenta apud Routh, Rel. Sacr. Vol. II. p. 6, and the notes on this passage,) who thus explains the opinions propounded by Cerinthus, on the ground of a pretended divine revelation: μετὰ τὴν ἀνάστασιν ἐπίγειον εἶναι τὸ βασίλειον τοῦ Χριστοῦ, καὶ πάλιν ἐπιθυμίαις καὶ ἡδοναῖς ἐν Ἰερουσαλὴμ τὴν σάρκα πολιτευομένην δουλένειν. Compare also Gennadius *De ecclesiasticis dogmatibus*, cap. 55. A learned account of the opinions of the ancients and moderns concerning the Millenium may be found in Mosheim *De rebus Christianorum ante Constantinum Magnum*, pp. 720—728; in Whitby, *Treatise on the true Millenium*; and in Mede's works, *passim*.]

way, namely, that we esteem and make the glorified bodies no more spiritual, than the perfectness, property, and truth of the bodies may permit and suffer: contrariwise, that we make them not altogether so carnal and unghostly, that it might be thought how that natural and frail bodies shall be in the glory[11]. Old writers say also, that Origen did not perfectly confess the resurrection of the flesh, but that in the resurrection he fantasied and imagined such a body, as hath little difference from a spirit. And therefore in *Definitionibus Ecclesiasticis* there is a chapter against the said Origen, in manner following: "If that which falleth do stand up again, then shall our flesh truly rise again: for the same falleth in very deed, and shall not come to nothing, as Origen's opinion was, that there should be made a sifting and change of the bodies, namely, that there should be given us a new body for the flesh; but even the same frail flesh that falleth of the just, and vanisheth, shall with our feebleness rise again, that because of sin it may suffer pain, or else, according to his deserts, continue in eternal honour and glory[12]."

Defin. Eccles. cap. 6.

[[11] Jerome speaks strongly against these opinions in different parts of his writings, and especially in those against Origen and John bishop of Jerusalem. The allusion in the text appears to be to a passage in his letter *Ad Pammachium et Oceanum de erroribus Origenis*, Epist. LXV. where to the heretics who denied the resurrection of the body, and who asked, Quid nobis prodest resurrectio, si fragile corpus resurget, et futuri angelorum similes habebimus et naturam? he answers: Dedignantur videlicet cum carne et ossibus resurgere, cum quibus resurrexit et Christus. In another letter (Epist. XXXVIII.) against the errors of John bishop of Jerusalem, he writes: Hæc est vera resurrectionis confessio, quæ sic gloriam carni tribuit, ut non auferat veritatem. See below, Chap. XX. p. 190.]

[[12] The work here referred to is a work of Gennadius, which has been improperly ascribed to Augustine, entitled, *Liber de definitionibus orthodoxæ fidei, sive ecclesiasticis dogmatibus*: Si id resurgere dicitur quod cadit, caro ergo nostra in veritate resurgit, sicut in veritate cadit. Et non secundum Origenem immutatio corporum erit, id est, aliud novum corpus pro carne: sed eadem caro corruptibilis, quæ cadit, tam justorum quam injustorum, incorruptibilis resurget, quæ vel pœnam sufferre possit pro peccatis, vel in gloria æterna manere pro meritis. August. Op. Tom. III. p. 45. D. Cave, Hist. Literaria. Vol. I. p. 376. Ed. 1688.]

CHAPTER XIX.

THE ERRORS OF ORIGEN CONCERNING THE RESURRECTION CONFUTED BY JEROME.

But forasmuch as I have once recited Origen's opinion touching the resurrection of the body, and somewhat recited the errors of some that denied the resurrection, declaring the scornful opinion of those whom they call Chiliasts[1]; I will shew now more largely what holy Jerome held of the resurrection of the dead, and how he confessed the true upright belief. He speaketh to Pammachius concerning the errors of John bishop of Jerusalem, and in the same writing he comprehendeth the doctrine and opinion of Origen concerning the resurrection in manner following. Origen saith, that "in the church there be sprung up two errors, the one from us, the other from the heretics; namely, that we, as the simple and lovers of the flesh, say, that even these bones, this blood, and this flesh, that is, that our face, members, and all the proportions of the body, and the whole body itself, shall rise again at the last day, so that we shall also go with the feet, work with the hands, see with the eyes, and hear with the ears." "This," saith he, "we speak as simple, homely, gross, and ignorant people. But the heretics, as Marcion, Apelles, Valentinus[2], and mad Manes, deny wholly and utterly the resurrection of the flesh, or body, giving salvation only unto the soul; and saying, that our words are nothing, when we affirm that, according to the ensample and pattern of our Lord Jesus Christ, we shall rise again; saying, that the Lord himself rose in a fantasy, or spirit, and that not only his resurrection, but also his birth came to pass more in the imagination, than in very truth;

Hierome ad Pammachium.

[1 With respect to the heretics, who denied the resurrection of the body, see Irenæus adv. Hær. Lib. v. cap. 2, p. 395. col. 2, and Dr Grabe's note ad loc. Ed. Oxf. 1702.]

[2 Compare Tertullian, *De Carne Christi*, cap. 1, and *passim;* also his treatise *De Resurrectione Carnis:* and for the opinions of the Manichees, August. Contra Faustum Manicheum, Lib. IV. Opera, Tom. VI. p. 48. K. Ed. 1541, and his works, *passim.*]

that is, that he was not born in very deed, but supposed to be born."

"Now for the opinion and mind of both these parties," Origen saith, "it pleased him not; namely, that he abhorreth the flesh on our side, and the fantasy on the heretics' part; for each of them doth too much: and namely they of our side, for that they would be again the same they were afore; and for the other, that they utterly deny the resurrection of the bodies[3]."

And after certain words doth Jerome set forth Origen's opinion, what he held of the resurrection, and saith: "There is promised us another body, namely, a spiritual and heavenly, that cannot be comprehended nor seen with eyes, nor having any weight, and that, according to the circumstance and diversity of the place that it shall be in, shall be changed[4]." And after certain words doth Jerome set forth the opinion of Origen yet more plainly, saying: "O ye simple, the resurrection of our Lord Jesus Christ ought not to deceive you, in that he shewed his hands and feet, stood on the sea shore, went over the field with Cleophas, and said he had flesh and bones. This body, that was not born of the seed of man, and of lust or pleasure of the flesh, is endued with greater

[[3] Dicit ergo Origenes...duplicem errorem versari in ecclesia, nostrorum et hæreticorum. Nos simplices et philosarcas dicere, quod eadem ossa et sanguis et caro, id est, vultus et membra totiusque compago corporis, resurgat in novissima die; scilicet ut pedibus ambulemus, operemur manibus, videamus oculis, auribus audiamus... Hæc nos innocentes et rusticos asserit dicere. Hæreticos vero, in quorum parte sunt Marcion, Apelles, Valentinus, Manes, nomen insaniæ, penitus et carnis et corporis resurrectionem negare, et salutem tantum tribuere animæ. Frustraque nos dicere ad similitudinem Domini resurrecturos, quum ipse quoque Dominus in phantasmate resurrexerit; et non solum resurrectio ejus, sed et ipsa nativitas τῷ δοκεῖν, id est, putative visa magis sit, quam fuerit. Sibi autem displicere utramque sententiam, fugere se et nostrorum et hæreticorum phantasmata; quia utraque pars in contrarium nimia sit; aliis idem volentibus se esse quod fuerunt; aliis resurrectionem corporis omnino denegantibus. Hieron. Epist. XXXVIII. ad Pammach. adv. errores Joannis Hierosol. Opera, Tom. IV. Pars 2, p. 320. Edit. Paris. 1693—1706.]

[[4] Aliud nobis spirituale et ætherium promittitur, quod nec tactui subjacet, nec oculis cernitur, nec pondere prægravatur, et pro locorum, in quibus futurum est, varietate mutabitur. Ib. pp. 321, 322.]

freedom than another body, and with his nature is not unlike the spiritual and heavenly body. For when the doors were shut he entered, and in breaking of bread vanished he away from their sight[1]," &c. But at the last, Jerome answereth unto Origen's foundation, and saith: "Like as he shewed his true hands and his true sides, so did he truly eat with them, went truly with Cleophas, spake to them truly with his mouth, sat truly at the table with them at supper, took the bread with his true hands, gave thanks, brake it, and reached it them. And whereas he immediately vanished out of their sight, that is ascribed to the power of God, and to no fantasy, or false body. When he afore his resurrection was brought out from Nazareth, that they might throw him down from the top of the hill, he passed through the midst of them, that is, he escaped out of their hands. May we then talk with Marcion, that his birth was therefore but a fantasy, because that he against nature escaped those that had him? How sayest thou? did they not know him in the way, when he yet had the body that he had afore? Upon this hear the scripture: 'Their eyes were holden, that they should not know him.' But was he any other when they knew him not, or was he any other when they knew him? Verily he was always one and like himself. And therefore to know, and not to know, is given to the eyes, and not to him that is seen, although it be ascribed unto him also, that he held their eyes, lest they should know him[2]."

The confutation of Origen's error.

[[1] Nec vos, O simplices, resurrectio Domini decipiat, quod latus et manus monstraverit, in litore steterit, in itinere cum Cleopha ambulaverit, et carnes et ossa habere se dixerit. Illud corpus aliis pollet privilegiis, quod de viri semine et carnis voluptate non natum est. Comedit post resurrectionem suam et bibit, et vestitus apparuit, tangendum se præbuit; ut dubitantibus apostolis fidem faceret resurrectionis. Sed tamen non dissimulat naturam aerei corporis et spiritualis. Clausis enim ingreditur ostiis, et in fractione panis ex oculis evanescit. Ib. p. 322.]

[[2] Quomodo veras manus et verum ostendit latus; ita vere comedit cum apostolis et discipulis; vere ambulavit cum Cleopha; vere lingua locutus est cum hominibus; vero accubitu discubuit in cœna; veris manibus accepit panem, benedixit ac fregit, et porrigebat illis. Quod autem ab oculis repente evanuit, virtus Dei est, non umbræ et phantasmatis. Alioquin et ante resurrectionem, quum eduxissent eum

Afterward with many words giveth he answer to that, that the Lord entered when the doors were shut[3]. Yet doth he briefly answer thereunto in his commentaries on the last chapter of Isaiah, and saith: "I marvel that some after Christ's ascension will give and measure him a body made of the air, and soon returned to air again, because the Lord by the power of his majesty came in to the apostles, when the doors were shut; considering that afore his resurrection also he went upon the water of the sea, permitting the same unto holy Peter, who at the first through faith walked upon the water, but afterward when he, being faint in faith, began to sink and go under, he said unto him, 'O thou of little faith, why hast thou doubted[4]?'" Thus much wrote Jerome against Origen, and many other more yet in this book written to Pammachius against John bishop of Jerusalem, which, because of greatness and length, I have omitted to put here in writing.

de Nazareth, ut præcipitarent de supercilio montis, transivit per medios, id est, elapsus est de manibus eorum. Numquid juxta Marcionem dicere possumus, quod ideo nativitas ejus in phantasmate fuerit, quia contra naturam qui tenebatur elapsus est?...Et quomodo, inquies, non cognoscebant eum in itinere, si ipsum habebat corpus quod ante habuit? Audi scripturam dicentem: *Oculi eorum tenebantur, ne eum agnoscerent.* Et rursum: *Aperti sunt oculi eorum,* inquit, *et cognoverunt eum.* Numquid alius fuit quando non agnoscebatur, et alius quando agnitus est? Certe unus atque idem erat. Cognoscere ergo et non cognoscere oculorum fuit, non ejus qui videbatur, licet et ipsius fuerit: oculos enim tenebat eorum, ne se cognoscerent. Ib. p. 328.]

[3 Ib. p. 329.]

[4 Miror quosdam aereum corpus, et paulatim in auras tenues dissolvendum, post resurrectionem introducere; quia Dominus potentiâ sua clausis ingressus est januis. Qui certe et ante resurrectionem pendulo super mare ambulavit incessu, et hoc ipsum apostolo præbuit Petro; ut qui fide ambulavit, infidelitate postea mergeretur, cui dictum est: *Quare dubitasti, modicæ fidei?* Hieron. Comment. Lib. XVIII. in Isai. Proph. cap. 66. Op. Tom. III. p. 514. Ed. Paris. 1693—1706.]

CHAPTER XX.

SAINT JEROME'S OPINION OF THE RESURRECTION OF THE FLESH.

YET in the same book hath the said Jerome set his own opinion touching the resurrection of the flesh, directing the oration unto Bishop John, and saying: "If you will now confess the resurrection of the flesh after the truth, and not after fantasy, as thou sayest, then look that unto the words which thou hast spoken to content the simple, that even in the body, wherein we die and are buried, we shall rise again, thou add these words also, and say, *Seeing the spirit hath not flesh and bones, as ye see me have:* and forasmuch as it was so distinctly spoken unto Thomas, *Put thy finger in my hands, and thy hand in my side, and be not faithless, but believing;* therefore say thou, that we also after the resurrection shall have even the same members that we daily use, yea, the very same flesh, blood, and bone; the works whereof the holy scripture condemneth and rejecteth, and not their nature. And this is the right and true acknowledging of the resurrection; which so giveth honour unto the flesh, that therewith it minisheth nothing the verity of the flesh[1]."

Afterward speaketh he yet more evidently: "I will freely confess, though ye wry your mouths at it, scratch your head, and scrape with your feet, yea, and though ye should stone me to death forthwith, yet will I manifestly and plainly acknow-

[1 Vis resurrectionem carnis veritate et non putative, ut loqueris, confiteri? Post illa, quibus audientium blanditus es auribus, quod in ipsis corporibus, in quibus mortui sumus et sepulti, resurgamus; hoc potius adjunge, et dic, *Quoniam spiritus carnem et ossa non habet, sicut me videtis habere;* et proprie ad Thomam: *Infer digitum tuum in manus meas, et manum tuam in latus meum, et noli esse incredulus, sed fidelis.* Sic et nos post resurrectionem eadem habebimus membra, quibus nunc utimur, easdem carnes, et sanguinem, et ossa; quorum in scripturis sanctis opera, non natura damnatur....Hæc est vera resurrectionis confessio, quæ sic gloriam carni tribuit, ut non auferat veritatem. Hieron. Epist. xxxviii. ad Pammach. adv. errores Joannis Hierosol. Opera, Tom. iv. p. 323. Ed. 1693—1706.]

ledge and confess the faith of the church or congregation of God; and boldly pronounce, that the right, profound, christian truth of the resurrection can utterly not be understood without flesh, bones, blood, and members. Where flesh, bones, blood, and members are, there must needs be a difference of kind, as of man and woman; and where these both are distinct the one from the other, there John must be John, and Mary must be Mary. But thou needest not be astonished at the matter, as though a wedding also were there to be kept in all the past, seeing that before they died they lived without the work of their kind, that is, without the act of marriage."

" It is promised us, that we shall be like unto the angels, that is, partakers of the salvation, in the which salvation the angels are without flesh and distinction of kind; and yet it is given unto us in our flesh and kind. Thus believeth my simplicity, and understandeth, that the kind must be understood, howbeit without the works of the kind; yea, that men must rise again, and so become like unto the angels of God."

"Neither ought the resurrection of members forthwith therefore to be esteemed unprofitable and superfluous, because they shall not do their office, but stand idle. For while we are yet in this life, we endeavour ourselves not to perform the works of our members. As for the comparison towards the angels, it is not a changing of men into angels, but it is an increasing of the immortality and glory[2]."

Thus much have I spoken of the confessions of holy Jerome.

[[2] Ego libere dicam, et quamquam torqueatis ora, trahatis capillum, applaudatis pede, Judæorum lapides requiratis, fidem ecclesiæ apertissime confitebor. Resurrectionis veritas sine carne et ossibus, sine sanguine et membris, intelligi non potest. Ubi caro et ossa et sanguis et membra sunt, ibi necesse est ut sexus diversitas sit. Ubi sexus diversitas est, ibi Joannes Joannes, et Maria Maria. Noli timere eorum nuptias, qui etiam ante mortem in sexu suo sine sexus opere vixerunt....Angelorum nobis similitudo promittitur; id est, beatitudo illa, in qua sine carne et sexu sunt angeli, nobis in carne et sexu nostro donabitur. Mea rusticitas sic credit, et sic intelligit sexum confiteri sine sexuum operibus; homines resurgere, et sic eos angelis adæquari. Nec statim superflua videbitur membrorum resurrectio, quæ caritura sint officio suo; quum adhuc in hac vita positi, nitamur opera non

CHAPTER XXI.

SAINT AUGUSTINE'S MIND OF THE RESURRECTION OF THE FLESH.

TOUCHING the resurrection of our flesh, not only did holy Jerome believe thus, who yet testifieth that he acknowledgeth and confesseth the universal christian faith; but also St Austin wholly agreeth unto St Jerome, and namely, Lib. II. Retractat. cap. 3. For in repeating and correcting certain points out of the thirty-second chapter in the book *De Agone Christiano*[1], he saith: "I said it shall not be flesh and blood, but an heavenly body. This ought no man to understand, that therefore there shall be no true substance of the flesh; but with the names of flesh and blood must the infirmity of the flesh and blood be understood[2]." Item, Lib. I. Retractat. cap. 17, in repeating and correcting certain points which he had written long afore in the book [Cap. 10.] *De fide et symbolo*: "In the time of the angelical change," saith he, "it shall not be flesh and blood, but only a body, &c." This I spake of the changing of earthy bodies into heavenly, &c. But if one would understand it so, that the earthy body which we now have should so in the resurrection be altered and changed, that these members and the substance of this flesh shall not remain, no doubt he is not in the right way, but ought better to be instructed, considering that he

implere membrorum. Similitudo autem ad angelos non hominum in angelos demutatio, sed profectus immortalitatis et gloriæ est. Ib. p. 325.]

[1 Opera, Tom. III. p. 175. E. Ed. 1541.]

[2 In quo illud quod positum est,—"Nec eos audiamus qui carnis resurrectionem futuram negant, et commemorant quod ait apostolus Paulus, Caro et sanguis regnum Dei non possidebunt, non intelligentes quod ipse dicit Apostolus, Oportet corruptibile hoc induere incorruptionem, et mortale hoc induere immortalitatem: cum enim hoc factum fuerit, jam non erit caro et sanguis, sed cœleste corpus," —non sic accipiendum est, quasi carnis non sit futura substantia, sed carnis et sanguinis nomine ipsam corruptionem carnis et sanguinis intelligendus est apostolus nuncupasse, quæ utique in regno illo non erit, ubi caro incorruptibilis erit. August. Retractat. Lib. II. cap. 3. Opera, Tom. I. p. 10. D.]

is warned and monished through the body of our Lord, which after the resurrection appeared even with the same members, not only that he might be seen with eyes, but handled also and touched with hands. Besides this he testifieth, that he hath true flesh upon him, when he saith, 'Handle me, and see: for a spirit hath not flesh and bones as ye see me have.' Therefore it is evident and plain, that the holy apostle Paul denied not, that the true substance of the flesh should be in the kingdom of God; but rather with these words, *flesh* and *blood*, he understood, that either men which live after the flesh should not have the inheritance of heaven, else that there should be in heaven no infirmity of the flesh at all. This is a grievous matter for unbelievers, and hardly are they persuaded to believe the resurrection; but most diligently, and after my power, have I treated thereof in the last book *De Civitate Dei*[3]."

Yet handleth he of the resurrection not only in the last book, but also in the thirteenth book *De Civitate Dei* he writeth thus: "The christian faith doubteth verily nothing at all to confess of our Saviour, that also after the resurrection, though now in the spiritual flesh, yet also in his true flesh he did eat and drink with his disciples. Hereof are they called also spiritual bodies; not that they therefore cease to be bodies, but that through the spirit which giveth

De Civitate Dei, Lib. XIII. cap. 22 et 23.

[[3] In hoc libro (scil. de Fide et Symbolo) cum de resurrectione carnis ageretur, "Resurget," inquam, "corpus"... Quod cui videtur incredibile, qualis sit nunc caro attendit; qualis autem tunc futura sit non considerat, quia illo tempore mutationis angelicæ non jam caro erit et sanguis, sed tantum corpus...Sed quisquis ea sic accipit, ut existimet ita corpus terrenum, quale nunc habemus, in corpus cœleste resurrectione mutari, ut nec membra ista nec carnis sit futura substantia; proculdubio corrigendus est, commonitus de corpore Domini, qui post resurrectionem in eisdem membris, non solum conspiciendus oculis, verum etiam manibus tangendus (al. tractandus) apparuit. Carnemque se habere etiam sermone firmavit, dicens: Palpate, et videte; quia spiritus carnem et ossa non habet, sicut me videtis habere. Unde constat apostolum non carnis substantiam negasse in Dei regno futuram; sed aut homines, qui secundum carnem vivunt, carnis et sanguinis nomine nuncupasse, aut ipsam corruptionem, quæ tunc utique nulla erit.....De qua re ad persuadendum infidelibus difficili, diligenter quantum potui me disseruisse reperiet, quisquis *De Civitate Dei* librum legerit novissimum. August. Retractat. Lib. I. cap. 17, Tom. I. p. 6. I.]

<small>And the same is again, Retractat. Lib. I. cap. 13.</small> life they shall be preserved and remain[1]." "For like as these our bodies which have a living soul, and yet be not named a spirit that giveth life, but natural or soulless bodies, and therefore are not souls, but bodies; so shall the glorified bodies be called spiritual. Yet God forbid we should therefore believe that they shall be spirits; but bodies shall they be, which shall have the substance of the flesh. And forasmuch as they are preserved and made alive through the spirit, they shall suffer no grief or infirmity. Then shall not man be earthy, but heavenly; not that the body which is made of the earth shall no more continue the same body, but that through the heavenly gift and grace he shall be so from henceforth, that being such a kind and nature as cannot perish, and altered from all infirmities, he shall be able to dwell commodiously in heaven[2]."

Furthermore saith St Austin in the twenty-second book, the thirtieth chapter: "How the bodies there shall move, I dare not rashly define; for I cannot comprehend it, it passeth my understanding. Yet shall their moving and state, even as also their proportion, be altogether beautiful; and howsoever it shall be, it shall be in the place where nothing can be but that which is beautiful and holy; yea, where the spirit will, there straight shall the body be also. Neither will the spirit any thing, that is not very seemly and comely both for him and it[3]." Thus have I hitherto recited St Augustine's belief, to conclude this matter of the resurrection.

[1 Fides Christiana de ipso Salvatore non dubitat, quod etiam post resurrectionem jam quidem in spiritali carne, sed tamen vera, cibum ac potum cum discipulis sumpsit. Non enim potestas, sed egestas edendi talibus corporibus auferetur. Unde et spiritalia erunt; non quia corpora esse desistent, sed quia spiritu vivificante subsistent. August. de Civ. Dei. Lib. XIII. cap. 22. Opera, Tom. v. p. 112. L.]

[2 Nam sicut ista, quæ habent animam viventem, nondum spiritum vivificantem, animalia dicuntur corpora, nec tamen animæ sunt, sed corpora: ita illa spiritalia vocantur corpora. Absit tamen ut spiritus ea credamus futura, sed corpora carnis habitura substantiam, sed nullam tarditatem corruptionemque carnalem spiritu vivificante passura. Tunc jam non terrenus, sed cœlestis homo erit; non quia corpus, quod de terra factum est, non ipsum erit, sed quia dono cœlesti jam tale erit, ut etiam cœlo incolendo, non amissa natura, sed mutata qualitate conveniat. Ib. cap. 23. p. 113. A.]

[3 Qui motus illic talium corporum sint futuri, temere definire

CHAPTER XXII.

WHAT AURELIUS PRUDENTIUS THOUGHT OF THE SAME.

I WILL hereunto add the verses of the excellent and christian man, Aurelius Prudentius, which do wonderfully express unto us the resurrection of our flesh, and set it before our eyes:

My body in Christ
   Shall rise again:
I speak it earnest;
   For it is plain.

Why wouldst thou then
   I should despair,
O flesh, when I
   Do see so far?

The way that Jesus
   Christ my Lord,
Went after his death,
   As saith his word;

This is the ground
   And foundation,
My heart believeth
   With confession:

That I am sure,
   And know certain,
My body shall rise
   Wholly again.

Not one be less
   Than was before,
Neither in greatness
   Any more:

With strength and shape,
   As it lived here,
Afore they it
   To grave did bear.

There is no tooth,
   Nor nail so small,
No ear so little,
   But though it fall,

Yet perish it shall
   Not finally,
But out of grave
   Rise certainly.

God which afore,
   Created me,
With shape and strength
   Undoubtedly,

Wherewith I here
   On earth should live,
No feeble nor weak
   Thing me shall give.

For where any thing
   Shall perish at all,
It is old, feeble—
   So do not then call

non audeo, quod excogitare non valeo. Tamen et motus et status, sicut ipsa species, decens erit, quicumque erit, ubi quod non decebit non erit. Certe ubi volet spiritus, ibi protinus erit corpus; nec volet aliquid spiritus, quod nec spiritum possit decere nec corpus. Ibid. Lib. XXII. cap. 30. Opera, Tom. v. p. 217. K.]

> Our bodies at the resurrection shall not be feeble nor weak.

Of our bodies
    The renovation.
Therefore is this
    My expectation;

What sickness, pain,
    And adversity,
What death, in this,
    Vale of misery,

Out of this world
    Now taketh away,
Shall, when I rise
    At the last day,

From death to life
    Anew certain
Be given me all
    Together again.

Forseeing that death
    Is overcome,
It ever beseemeth
    Us all and some,

Quietly to trust
    With stedfastness,
Our God will keep
    With us promise;

Lest when we come
    Into the grave,
A man no hope
    Then after have;

When he to life
    Cometh eternal,
That he for his
    Body mortal,

Which here so full
    Of faultes was,
As brittle and frail
    As any glass,

Shall have a body
    Of perfectness,
That cold can not
    Nor hunger press;

Though weakness be
    At all season
The strength of death
    And operation.

Thereby in us
    What is consumed,
When it again
    Shall be restored;

Then through the power
    Whereby we rise,
We go to the Father
    In perfect wise.

This should right well
    Content our heart;
Therefore my body
    Regardeth no smart.

In Christ my trust
    Is constantly,
Who promiseth us
    Assuredly,

To raise us up
    From earth at last:
Therefore be thou
    Nothing aghast,

For sickness nor
    Adversity;
Nor yet let thou
    The grave fear thee.

Let this ever
    Thy comfort be,
That Christ prepareth
    The way for thee;

> Wherein himself
> Is gone before:
> Follow thou, and live
> For evermore[1].

CHAPTER XXIII.

THE BODIES OF UNBELIEVERS SHALL VERILY RISE AGAIN.

But to the intent that no man doubt touching the resurrection of the flesh of the unbelievers, I will bring forth certain testimonies of holy scripture, which do manifestly declare that the unbelievers, or ungodly, shall with their own true bodies rise again. The prophet Isaiah, in the last chapter of his book, saith: "They shall go forth and look *Isai. lxvi.* upon the bodies of them that have vilely behaved themselves against me: for their worms shall not die, neither shall their fire be quenched, and all flesh shall abhor them." With

[[1] Nosco meum in Christo corpus consurgere: quid me
Desperare jubes? veniam quibus ille revenit
Calcata de morte viis. Quod credimus hoc est.
Et totus veniam, nec enim minor aut alius quam
Nunc sum, restituar: vultus, vigor, et color idem
Qui modo vivit, erit; nec me vel dente vel ungue
Fraudatum removet patefacti fossa sepulchri.
Qui jubet ut redeam, non reddet debile quicquam;
Nam si debilitas redit, instauratio non est.
Quod casus rapuit, quod morbus, quod dolor hausit,
Quod truncavit edax senium, populante veterno,
Omne revertenti reparata in membra redibit.
Debet enim mors victa fidem, ne fraude sepulchri
Reddat curtum aliquid; quamvis jam curta voraris
Corpora, debilitas tamen et violentia morbi
Virtus mortis erat, reddet quod particulatim
Sorbuerat quocunque modo, ne mortuus omnis
Non redeat, si quid pleno de corpore desit.
Pellite corde metum, mea membra, et credite vosmet
Cum Christo reditura Deo; nam vos gerit ille
Et secum revocat: morbos ridete minaces,
Inflictos casus contemnite, tetra sepulchra
Despuite; exsurgens quo Christus provocat, ite.
Aurel. Prudent. Apotheosis. De resurrectione carnis humanæ. Opera, p. 38. Ed. Paris. 1687.]

this sentence doth the prophet play, after the manner and custom of those that have soon gotten the victory; which with great desire, after the battle is won, get them out of the city into the field, to view and look upon the bodies of such as are slain, and how fortunately they have fought. Forasmuch now as Christ also hath fought prosperously, overcome his enemies on dooms-day, and made them his footstool, the faithful shall go out to see the bodies of the ungodly. The prophet doth for this cause call them bodies, even to declare, that the bodies raised up from death shall be very true flesh. He continueth further also in the recited sentence, and saith, "Their worms shall not die:" for the bodies, or corpses, are full of worms, neither are they aught but worm's meat.

All this is spoken after the custom and property of man, and weakness of this time; and herewith is described unto us, and set before our eyes, eternal punishment, and how it shall go in the life to come.

Dan. xii.
In Daniel we read thus: "Many of them that sleep in the dust of the earth shall awake, some to everlasting life, some to perpetual shame and reproof." The whole multitude of bodies, saith he, that are become dust, yea, all flesh shall through the power of God rise again, but not in like case and sort: for the good shall arise to eternal life, the evil to everlasting death.

John v.
After this manner spake the Lord also: "Verily, verily, I say unto you, the hour cometh, in the which all they that are in the graves shall hear his voice, and shall come forth; they that have done good to life, and they that have done evil to death." Who is so ignorant but he perceiveth, that to sleep in the earth, as the prophet Daniel said, and to be in the graves, as Christ said, is one manner of speech, and of like effect? Now forasmuch as they that are in the dust of the earth, and in the graves, come forth and rise again, and only the bodies are in the graves wherein they corrupt; it followeth that men's true bodies, not only of the good, but also of the evil, shall truly rise again. And the same doth the Lord yet declare more evidently, Matth. x.: "Fear not ye them that kill the body, and are not able to kill the soul; but rather fear him, which may destroy soul and body into hell." Not only the souls, but also the bodies of unbelievers

doth the Lord destroy. Out of the which it followeth, that they shall rise again: for if they should not rise again, they could not be tormented and plagued. Neither shall any other body rise again to pain and punishment, but even the same that with his vile works hath deserved the plague.

And hereunto serveth also the description of the last judgment, Matth. xxv. And St Paul saith, 2 Cor. v. "We must all appear before the judgment-seat of Christ, that every one may receive in his body according as he hath done, whether it be good or bad." See how manifestly and expressly the holy apostle testifieth, that the body shall rise again.

In the same terrible judgment of God, saith he, must every one take his body to him again. And why must he take the body upon him again? Even to the intent, that when any one hath received his body again, he may likewise receive the reward that he by and with his living body hath deserved. Now hath the body something to do with godliness and ungodliness, with virtue and vice: for the body is an instrument or vessel, wherewith somewhat is done, and therefore in the last judgment of God the body, according to the divine righteousness, shall not be omitted, neither forgotten at all. For if it have been obedient and subject unto the Spirit, if it have suffered much trouble for the name of Jesus Christ, if it hath been an earnest follower of righteousness, then shall it be worthy also to be glorified. Again, if it hath been given over to worldly voluptuous pleasures, or transitory things of this world, then with the soul that wrought with it shall it justly go to eternal damnation. Therefore the unbelievers shall truly rise again in their own flesh; yea, even in the same, which they here in this time have fed and pampered with all voluptuous pleasure and excess. And like as they in this time have with their body taken their own pleasure, joy, and delight; so in the life to come they shall be plagued and punished with everlasting pain and torment in the same body.

For St Paul witnesseth further in the Acts of the Apostles, and saith: "I worship the God of my fathers, believing Acts xxiv. all things which are written in the law and the prophets, and have hope towards God, that the same resurrection of the dead, which they themselves look for, shall be of the just and unjust.

<small>De Fide ad Petrum, cap. v.</small> Therefore holy Augustine, in the book *De fide ad Petrum Diaconum*, said well and christianly, according to the nature of the apostle's doctrine: "The unrighteous shall have a common resurrection of the flesh with the righteous; but the grace of the change, or glorification, they shall not have. For frailty and misery shall not be taken away from the bodies of the ungodly, neither the shame and reproach, sickness and feebleness, in the which they are sown; which therefore through death are not extinct and taken away, that they may belong to eternal death, pain, and punishment, everlastingly to be plagued, body and soul, with continual torment that never ceaseth[1]." These are Augustine's words. And after like <small>John v.</small> sort did the Lord also say in the gospel: "They that have done evil shall rise to the resurrection of judgment, or damnation." As if he would say, The ungodly that with their bodies shall rise again, shall rise with such property and proportion of their body, that their bodies may suffer the pain and torment, namely that they, now being made everlasting, may not be wasted and consumed away through any pain or trouble, how great and horrible soever it be. And so the bodies of the ungodly that rise again from death, shall after the said manner be altered and changed. For the bodies, that might afore through pain or trouble be broken and consumed, are now altogether as iron, yea, such as cannot be broken, and yet painful and passible; so that from henceforth the more they be tormented, the harder they become, and through God's vengeance more unapt to be destroyed, and yet made the more able to suffer misery.

[[1] Habebunt ergo iniqui cum justis resurrectionem carnis communem; immutationis tamen gratiam non habebunt, quæ dabitur justis. Quoniam a corporibus impiorum non auferetur corruptio, et ignobilitas, et infirmitas in quibus seminantur; quæ ob mortem non extinguentur, ut illud juge tormentum corpori atque animæ sit mortis æternæ supplicium. August. de Fide ad Petrum Diac. cap. 3. Opera, Tom. III. p. 51. B. Ed. 1541.—This is not a genuine work of Augustine: it belongs to Fulgentius. See Cave, Hist. Lit. Vol. I. p. 385.]

THE

THIRD PART OF THIS BOOK,

ENTITLED

THE HOPE OF THE FAITHFUL,

TOUCHING THE DAMNED'S PERDITION AND THE
BLESSED'S SALVATION.

CHAPTER XXIV.

THE DEATH AND DAMNATION OF THE UNGODLY.

Now seeing the onset is given and the oration come so far, I must also speak somewhat of the eternal death and damnation of the unbelievers, that this matter may be wholly, uprightly, and perfectly brought to an end. I will therefore briefly declare, that the death and damnation of the unbelievers and ungodly is enjoined unto them of God. Item, that the souls are passible. Moreover, where the scripture declareth the place of damnation to be, and after what sort damnation shall torment the unbelievers. Finally, I will declare, whether the punishment of the ungodly be everlasting, or whether it shall cease at length.

Holy scripture doth oft and many times make mention of the death of the soul; which yet concerneth not the substance, but the state thereof. For holy Augustine in his book *De Fide et Symbolo* speaketh thereof very well and christianly: "Like as the soul," saith he, "by reason of vices and wicked manners is frail, so may it also be called mortal. For the death of the soul is to fall from God, and not to keep itself unto God: which is also the first sin committed in paradise, as it is contained in holy scripture[2]." Moreover the soul dieth, when it is verily

The death of the soul.

De Fide et Symbolo. cap. 10.

[2 Potest enim et anima, sicut corruptibilis propter morum vitia, ita etiam mortalis dici. Mors quippe animæ est apostatare a Deo, quod primum ejus peccatum in paradiso sacris literis continetur. August. de Fide et Symb. cap. 10. Opera, Tom. III. p. 34. H.]

spoiled of eternal life, and cast into everlasting sorrow, trouble, and misery; and therefore saith Augustine further: "The soul also hath her death, namely, when it lacketh and is destitute of the eternal and godly life, which truly and justly is called the life of the soul: but undeadly or immortal is it called, because it never ceaseth to live, how miserable soever the life of it be. What bodily death is, every man knoweth well; but eternal death, when a man dieth the second time, is this, when the flesh riseth again, and so is placed in everlasting torment. For after the last sentence or judgment of God the whole man, and not the half, shall be either saved or damned[1]." The eternal death also hath St John in his Revelation called the second death. This is appointed because of sin, and is not a resting or ceasing, but a continual pain. This death is called also damnation, that is, a judgment; because the ungodly is adjudged unto pain, and for that there is appointed him a torment, sorrow, and trouble that never ceaseth, and that, as touching the greatness thereof, can never be expressed with tongue.

Rev. ii. 20.

CHAPTER XXV.

THAT THERE IS AN ETERNAL DEATH AND DAMNATION, AND THAT THE SOUL IS PASSIBLE.

Now that there is an eternal damnation, the truth and righteousness of God testifieth. For how could God be righteous, if he had no punishment wherewith to torment and plague the vicious and wicked? Therefore out of doubt an eternal death and damnation there is, though the ungodly do mock and laugh it to scorn, and pause not upon it.

The godly sacred bible, which is an assured witness of the truth, saith evidently: "Death is the stipend, or reward of sin." And, "By one man came sin into the world, and by sin death." Item, "Through the sin of one man is the evil fallen by inheritance, and come upon all men unto

Rom. vi.

Rom. vii.

[[1] The substance of this passage is found in De Civ. Dei: Lib. XIII. cap. 2. Opera, Tom. v. p. 108. C—E.]

damnation:" for in the book of Genesis God saith: "In what day soever thou eatest of this tree, thou shalt die the death." Now did he eat thereof, and therefore he also died, and was even condemned, appointed, and adjudged unto eternal death. The Lord saith also in the Gospel: "If ye believe not that it is I, ye shall die in your sins." Item, "He that believeth not is condemned already." Such like testimonies are found in holy scripture innumerable; out of the which we finally conclude, that death and damnation is enjoined, appointed, and adjudged of God unto all unbelievers and ungodly. Gen. iii.
John viii.
John iii.

But forasmuch as there be some which think, that seeing the soul is a spirit, it cannot, neither may suffer, yea, that it is not subdued unto any passion at all; therefore against such curious teachers I will set now the soul of the gorgeous rich man in the Gospel, which expressly and plainly saith: "O send Lazarus, that he may dip the tip of his finger in water, and cool my tongue: for I am tormented in this flame." Lo, the rich man's soul is tormented in the fire. Hereon now it followeth, that the souls are passible, and subject to suffer. And though this be shewed us of the Lord as a parable, yet it is done for this intent, even to describe and to declare unto us the state and case of the souls that are separated from the bodies. And how pain and punishment is appointed unto the souls, it is found expressed, not only in the similitudes, but also in the holy Gospel of Matthew. The truth itself saith: "Fear ye him rather, which may destroy soul and body into hell." [Matt. x.] What the mouth of God speaketh must needs be true: yea, a shameful and strange thing were it for any man henceforth to doubt in this, that with so evident testimonies is witnessed. We ought rather to beware, that with our vicious life we deserve not to learn and feel by experience the righteous judgment of God, concerning the which we now doubt and demand so foolishly, as though there shall be nothing of it. Now what I have spoken of the souls already departed from the body, must be understood also of the bodies which come again to the souls in the resurrection.

CHAPTER XXVI.

THE BODIES OF THE UNBELIEVERS BEING RAISED ARE PASSIBLE.

For that the bodies, which come again to the souls, and are raised up, are passible, it may well be understood and perceived by that which is treated of already.

St Augustine, Lib. XXI. *De Civitate Dei*, cap. 4[1]. sheweth by many natural examples and evidences, that living bodies may well remain and continue in the fire. But touching the place of the punishment, or where the souls with their bodies shall be tormented, the scripture saith simply and plainly, that the unbelievers go down into hell. Hereof is it easy to perceive, that hell is under us in the earth: notwithstanding to go about to describe, to shew and compare precisely the place and the room where it lieth, and to print it, becometh not us verily, but is a foolish presumption. The testimonies of the scripture are simple and plain. For the prophet David saith: "Let death fall suddenly upon them, and let them go down quick into hell; for wickedness is in their houses and privy chambers." Item, "With all their substance went they down quick into hell, and the earth covered them, and they perished from out of the congregation." Hereunto serveth also right well the destruction of Sodom, and that which the prophet Ezekiel declareth, namely, that all cruel people are gone down and descended into hell; as the Elamites, which are the Persians, Edomites, and others: and therefore concludeth he farther, that even Pharao the king of Egypt, seeing that he also is a tyrant, must be thrust down into hell, and be gathered unto other uncircumcised, that is to say, unbelievers.

Item, in Luke is the hell placed beneath, downwards: for thus is it written in the evangelist: "Between us and you there is a great space set; so that they which would go down from hence to you cannot." The holy apostle Peter, speaking of the angels that fell, saith evidently, that they are cast down into hell, kept, and bound with the

Psalm lv.

Numb. xvi.

Gen. xix.

Ezek. xxxii.

Luke xvi.

2 Peter ii.

[[1] August. Opera, Tom. IV. p. 198. B. G. Ed. 1541.]

chains of darkness for ever. Isaiah also speaketh of hell, and saith: "The Lord hath set hell in the deep, and made it wide." As for the manner, fashion, and measure of the damnation, and how great the torment of hell is upon unbelievers, I suppose no tongue is able to express the terrible and hugesome pain and punishment thereof; for Virgil the old poet, though he were an heathen man, yet when he had recited divers and sundry vices, and what punishment is ordained for them of God, he said, in the sixth book of his Æneid: *Isai. xxx.* *Virgilius.*

> An hundred tongues,
> And mouths as many
> Although I had,
> With eloquence high;
> And though my voice
> All iron were
> In strength; yet could
> I not declare
> The vices of men,
> Nor yet can tell,
> What pains therefore
> They suffer in hell[2].

CHAPTER XXVII.

THE PAINS OF HELL AND THE MATTER FOR THE CONTINUANCE OF THE TORMENTS, WITH THE SPACE OF THE PLACE, AND KINDS OF PUNISHMENTS.

YEA, though the holy scripture itself cannot with sufficient words express the pains of hell and punishment of the damned, yet doth it partly describe the same with outward and corporal things; giving us occasion thereby to consider far greater things, and, so to say, out of the small

[2 Virgil Æneid. Lib. VI. 624—626:
  Non, mihi si linguæ centum sint, oraque centum,
  Ferrea vox, omnes scelerum comprendere formas,
  Omnia pœnarum percurrere nomina possim.]

to ponder and weigh the greater. As when it calleth the pains of hell the outward darkness, that is, most terrible sorrow and trouble; calling the pain also weeping and gnashing of teeth. Item, cold, and continual fire, that never quencheth, and the perpetual gnawing worm; as every one that hath read the gospel is well informed. The prophet Ezekiel saith, that in hell there is a great multitude of graves; and so by a figurative and borrowed speech he declareth the horror, mourning, weeping, and lamentation of the damned. The Greeks in their language named hell of darkness, cold, trembling, and quaking. For Hades cometh of *a* and εἴδειν, that is, *of not seeing;* or *Tartarus,* of the word *tartarizein,* that is, *to shudder for cold,* or of *taratto,* that is, *to be in heaviness, put in fear,* or *out of quiet.* But for the opening of this matter we will take the testimonies of the scripture in hand again. The Lord saith: "At the end of the world shall the Son of man send forth his angels, and they shall gather out of his kingdom all things that offend, and them which do iniquity, and shall cast them into the fiery oven; there shall be wailing and gnashing of teeth." And even the said words doth the Lord use again in the same evangelist. Item, Isaiah saith: "For he from the beginning hath prepared Tophet, that is, hell, even for kings; and hath made it deep and wide. The mansions or chambers thereof are of fire and exceeding much wood, which the breath of the Lord, as a river of brimstone, doth kindle." The place of the prophet have I partly declared in the exposition of the fifth chapter of Matthew, and here will I now partly expound it.

The prophet truly with these words declareth an assured, and a very wide and broad place of hell, when he saith: "He hath made it deep and wide." Hereof then it followeth, that hell is in the depth, and that the place itself is an horrible depth; for that whoso doth once sink down into it, shall come no more thereout: neither needeth any man to think that the place is not great and wide enough; for touching wideness, it shall be able enough to hold all damned persons. "For the wideness and greatness thereof," saith the prophet, "is exceeding horrible." The terrible pain and torment, wherewith the ungodly are punished, hath the prophet described with these words, and said: "The mansions and chambers thereof are of fire." As if he would say: "The pain of hell is greater than can be expressed; for the fire noteth an unoutspeakable trouble." As for stuff to be tormented withal, it shall never lack, neither shall the pain have ever any end. Therefore saith he, that "there is much wood." It followeth moreover, that the Lord's breath, which is as a river of brimstone, doth kindle, and as a bellows blow the fire, quickening it, and ever renewing it to burn evermore. Therefore we ought not to think that that fire is kept in by natural causes; for by the power of God is it kindled and kept in. The same prophet saith also: "They shall go forth, and look upon the bodies or corses of them that have vilely behaved themselves against me; for their worms shall not die, neither shall their fire be quenched, and all flesh shall abhor them." And unto these words hath the Lord respect, when he saith in the Gospel of Mark: "Better is it for thee to go halt or lame into life, than having two feet to be cast into hell, into the fire that never shall be quenched; where their worm never dieth, and their fire never goeth out." [Isai. lxvi.] [Mark ix.]

Herein therefore consisteth the punishment and damnation, that the ungodly, which here upon earth would not know God and receive the light of the gospel, shall be cast out from the face of God, wherein only yet is the fulness and perfectness of all joy; and then shall they be shut up in the great thick and perpetual darkness. For the Judge commandeth them to depart from him, and to go into the eternal pain and damnation. Yea, the ungodly shall go into themselves, and shall know the equity of the Judge; and therefore fret and gnaw their own heart with sighing, with unspeakable pain, great sorrow, and trouble. This is called, and so it is indeed, the gnawing worm that in the hearts of the ungodly never dieth. For St Paul saith plainly, that "at the righteous judgment of God the consciences of all men shall bear witness, and that the thoughts in themselves shall either accuse or excuse them." The same St Paul also, speaking of the judgment of God, saith: "Praise, honour, and immortality shall be given unto them that continue in good doing, and seek eternal life: but unto them that are rebellious, disobeying the truth, and follow iniquity, shall come indignation and wrath, trouble and anguish." [Rom. ii.]

Besides all this shall the ungodly be in the fellowship of most foul spirits, with whom they had their lust in this life. There shall all be full of confusion, loathsome and great torment, and so shall all burn together for eternity. For thus shall the Judge give sentence with plain and express words: *Matth. xxv.* "Depart from me, ye cursed, into everlasting fire, which is prepared for the devil and his angels." The prophet [Dan. xii.] Daniel saith also: "The wicked shall rise to perpetual shame and rebuke." Item, Isaiah: "All flesh shall abhor them." And holy scripture saith, that the ungodly are given over to the devil to burn perpetually.

CHAPTER XXVIII.

THE REFUTATION OF THEM THAT DENIED THE PUNISHMENT OF THE UNGODLY TO BE ETERNAL.

MOREOVER St Augustine saith in the last book *De Civitate Dei*[1], that some heretofore have been so merciful, that they durst promise grace, deliverance, and life, even unto those that are damned, and adjudged unto eternal death. The same witnesseth also St Jerome in his writing upon the last chapter of Isaiah[2]. But no man ought to be moved by such a foolish and erroneous opinion of certain unbelievers; which opinion hath of all faithful men been ever still rejected and condemned. For the testimonies or witness of the scripture, which wholly without all contradiction are to be credited, speak simply and plainly, that the punishment and damnation of the ungodly or unbelievers is everlasting; and not only of long continuance, as some expound it, but so *Isai. xxxiv.* great, that it cannot be expressed, and so perpetual, that it is without end. Hereupon, for the opening of the matter, we will shew more testimonies. Isaiah saith: "Thy rivers

[1 Lib. XXI. cap. 17. Opera, Tom. V. p. 202. I. K. Ed. 1541.]
[2 Hieron. Comment. Lib. XVIII. in Isai. Proph. cap. LXVI. Opera, Tom. III. p. 514. Ed. 1706.]

shall become resin, and the dust brimstone, the earth burning pitch, not able to be quenched day nor night. The smoke shall eternally go up; from generation to generation shall there be a destruction; neither shall any man be able to walk there in everlasting eternity." The prophet doubtless speaketh of hell, minding with many words to declare, that the punishment and pain of hell is eternal and without end. For first he saith: "Day and night shall it not quench?" then saith he further: "The smoke shall go up for evermore." Item, yet more plainly: "From generation to generation shall there be a destruction;" namely, a dwelling, wherein is nothing but pain and undoing. And at the end he addeth: "Neither shall any man be able to walk there in the everlasting eternity:" which is such a manner of speech, that scarce there can be any other found, that more distinctly, evidently, and plainly expresseth the eternity. For what is the everlasting eternity else, but a time without end? But to be able to dwell or walk there signifieth not, that no man shall dwell in hell; but that it is a loathsome horrible place, wherein every man desireth neither to dwell, nor walk.

Other prophets also, speaking of the destruction of lands and cities, have with such like manner of speech described a very foul and horrible subversion. Therefore would the holy prophet Isaiah also express here nothing else, but an everlasting loathsomeness, that never ceaseth.

In the holy prophet Daniel it is written thus: "They that have instructed the multitude unto godliness, shall shine as the stars *in seculum et in perpetuum*, for ever and ever." Now lest by this word *seculum* any man understand a long season, as an hundred, or a thousand, or ten thousand years, he addeth thereto immediately, *in perpetuum*, that is, to the eternity, or for evermore. And like as the eternity is appointed for the righteous, so is there an everlasting eternity ordained for the wicked. For the Lord saith plainly: "They that have done good shall come forth to the resurrection of life, and they that have done evil to the resurrection of judgment." Note here the manner of speech, "to the resurrection of life, and to the resurrection of judgment." Now have I shewed afore, that this saying, "to rise up unto the resurrection of judgment," is as much as to rise to a continual

Dan. xii.

John v.

and still remaining state, in the which the bodies raised up endure perpetually in torment. We find also the like in the same gospel of John, that the Lord saith: "Whoso believeth on the Son hath eternal life; but he that believeth not the Son shall not see life, but the wrath of God abideth upon him." Lo, what could be more evidently and pithily spoken? "He shall not see life," saith the Lord. Item, "the wrath of God remaineth upon him." If he shall not see life, how shall he then, as yonder men say, be preserved or saved? Item, if "the wrath of God abide upon him," then surely the vengeance, which is the pain and punishment, shall not be taken away from him. And note that he saith: "The wrath of God abideth, yea, abideth on him." As if he would say, the punishment hangeth upon him, sticketh fast, moveth not away, altereth not, but worketh in the unbelievers without ceasing for evermore.

<small>John iii.</small>

The Lord saith: "All sins shall be forgiven the children of men, and also the blasphemies wherewith they blaspheme; but whoso blasphemeth the Holy Ghost, hath no forgiveness for evermore, but is guilty of eternal judgment." "For evermore," saith he, "hath he no remission." And hereunto he addeth: "He is in danger of eternal judgment;" that is, he shall be punished with everlasting continual punishment. The Lord saith moreover in the same evangelist: "Better it is for thee to enter into life halt or lame, than having two feet to be cast into hell fire, the fire that never quencheth, where their worm dieth not and their fire goeth not out." Wherein he repeateth once again, "the fire never quencheth," and addeth thereto, that "the worm never dieth." Wherefore, as the bodies ever continue, so endureth their worm also perpetually. For the worm liveth and is sustained only of the body or carrion. St John also saith in his Revelation: "If any man worship the beast and his image, and receive his mark in his forehead, or in his hand, the same shall drink the wine of the wrath of God, which is poured in the cup of his wrath; and he shall be punished in fire and brimstone before the holy angels and before the Lamb. And the smoke of their torment ascendeth up for evermore, and they have no rest day nor night, &c." And the like is repeated in the twentieth chapter.

<small>Mark iii.</small>

<small>Mark ix.</small>

<small>Rev. xiv.</small>

Thus much of eternal damnation.

CHAPTER XXIX.

OF ETERNAL LIFE AND SALVATION, AND THAT THERE IS AN ETERNAL LIFE.

Now resteth, that in the end of this book we collect somewhat out of the scripture concerning everlasting life and the most perfect salvation of all elect, which is our only expectation and only hope that we undoubtedly look for, and trust to inherit; and that through the benefits and merits of our Lord Jesus Christ. That there is a blessed and eternal life, no man can deny, unless he be altogether an enemy of God, and except there be in him no life at all. For if there be no everlasting life and no everlasting salvation, then is there also no God; or, though there were one, yet were he neither true nor just, seeing that to all righteous and faithful he hath promised eternal life. But a God there is, who is true and righteous: therefore is there also an eternal life and salvation, which he hath promised to faithful believers. This doth holy scripture record with these witnesses. David saith: "I believe and trust to see the riches of the Lord." And in the gospel the Lord saith: "Come, ye blessed of my Father, and possess the kingdom, which hath been prepared for you from the beginning of the world." Item: "O thou good and faithful servant, that hast been faithful in a little, I will make thee ruler over much. Enter into the joy of thy Lord." Paul also saith: "If we have a sure hope in Christ Jesus only in this life, then are we of all people the most wretched." And in many words to the Hebrews treateth he of the everlasting rest. But in the second chapter he speaketh of the hope of the faithful: "They desire a better country, that is to say, an heavenly." Item, Hebrews xiii: "We have here no remaining city, but we seek one for to come." For holy scripture calleth eternal life the kingdom of God, the kingdom of the Father, the native country of heaven, the joy of the Lord, the blessed rest and everlasting life. St Peter speaketh very evidently and plain: "Praised be God, the

[margin: Psalm xxvii. Matt. xxv. 1 Cor. xv. Heb. iv. Heb. xi. 1 Pet. i.]

Father of our Lord Jesus Christ, which according to his abundant mercy hath begotten us again unto a lively hope, by the resurrection of Jesus Christ from death, to an inheritance immortal, undefiled, and that perisheth not, reserved in heaven for you, which are kept by the power of God through faith unto salvation," &c.

CHAPTER XXX.

WHERE THE PLACE OF THE FAITHFUL IS.

YET are there some that ask, where the region or place of the blessed and faithful believers is? Of this have all virtuous and godly men had ever one opinion, namely, that the dwelling of the living shall be with God, according to that which the Lord saith in the gospel: "Blessed are they which be of a pure heart: for they shall see God." And though God be every where, yet will he not be seen in this time, but principally in the time to come, and in heaven, according as Moses hath written: "No man shall be able to see God and live." Therefore is it necessary for us to depart out of this time, and to be brought elsewhere, namely, to the place that is above us; where "God dwelleth in a light that no man can attain unto," as Paul saith: for there will he be perfectly seen of his. In St Luke it is read, that Abraham's lap or bosom is above in the height, but the harbour or dwelling of the damned beneath in the depth. It is found also, that Elias was in a fiery chariot taken hence, and carried upwards into heaven. And in John doth our Lord Jesus Christ pray, saying: "Father, those whom thou hast given me, I will that where I am, they also be there with me, that they may see mine honour and glory." But in this that I have treated of afore, it is manifestly declared, that the heaven is the same room and place of Jesus Christ, into the which he is bodily taken up in his glory. Whereof then it followeth of necessity, that the heaven, into which Christ ascended with his true body, is

<small>Matth. v.</small>

<small>[Exod. xxxiii.]</small>

<small>1 Tim. vi.</small>

<small>2 Kings ii.</small>
<small>John xvii.</small>

even the same place and rest, that faithful believers are taken up into. And into the same heaven desired Stephen to be received, when he lift up his eyes into heaven, and saw at the right hand of the Father Jesus standing; to whom he committed his soul, and said, "O Lord Jesus, receive my spirit."

CHAPTER XXXI.

HOW THE SALVATION SHALL BE.

But what the same life, and of what sort, fashion, and manner the salvation of the faithful shall be, or what the elect do or occupy in heaven, can of mortal men not perfectly be spoken. For St Augustine also in his twenty-second book *De Civitate Dei*, cap. 29, saith: "If I will say the truth, I cannot tell after what manner the operation, rest, and quietness of the blessed in heaven shall be. For the peace of God excelleth and passeth all understanding[1]." And likewise speaketh also St Paul out of the prophet, concerning the quality, fashion, and manner of eternal life: "The eye hath not seen, and the ear hath not heard, neither have entered into the heart of man, the things which God hath prepared for them that love him." Wherefore touching the excellency of eternal life, though all were spoken that the tongues of men were able, yet should it be hard for them to attain, and by words to express, the least and smallest portion thereof. For albeit we hear that the kingdom of Christ be filled with glory, joy, and salvation, yet the things that are named continue still far from our understanding; yea, they remain wrapped, as it were, in a dark speech and in a mist, until the day come, wherein he will open and give unto us his glory. Therefore when the holy prophets could with no words express the spiritual salvation, as it is in itself, yet,

De Civitate Dei, Lib. xxii. cap. 29.

1 Cor. ii. Isai. lxiv.

[1 Illa quidem actio, vel potius quies et otium, quale futurum sit, si verum velim dicere, nescio....Ibi enim est pax Dei, quæ, sicut ait apostolus, superat omnem intellectum. August. de Civ. Dei, Lib. xxii. cap. 29. Opera, Tom. v. p. 216. L. ed. 1541.]

as much as was possible they described, and set it forth by outward and bodily things. Therefore we may also, I suppose, by outward and corporal things get up, as it were, by steps to things invisible, and purchase unto ourselves an understanding of spiritual and everlasting good things. For St Paul to the Romans, speaking of the knowledge of the true, only, and eternal God, saith, that "God's invisible things, namely, his eternal power and Godhead, are understood, if his works be pondered and considered." And out of the good things that here upon earth are given unto men, hath the poet Marcellus very goodly and well concluded and counted, that the good things which for the blessed are prepared in the life to come, shall be such as now cannot be considered and expressed; and thus he saith:

Rom. i.

Marcellus de Piscibus[1].

O heaven, that art
   The throne most high,
A beautiful crown,
   Fair and worthy;
How wonderful, pure,
   And excellent,
Art thou beset
   In firmament
With stars, with sun,
   And moon doubtless,
Replete with joy,
   And much gladness;
Which God for us
   Hath prepared,

And cattle to give
   Hath not spared;
Waters and wood,
   With many a hill,
Vineyards, meadows,
   Fair fields to till,
Pleasant on earth,
   And commodious:
Thy dwelling, O Lord,
   How precious
Is it, all full of
   Honour and glory
For thy celestial
   Hast with thee.

Moreover holy scripture speaketh very simply and plainly, that eternal life consisteth herein, that we shall see God, and have the fruition of him, in whom is the fulness of all good, and without whom nothing can be desired or found

[1 The person who is here apparently referred to, is Marcellus Sidetes, a physician of Side in Pamphylia, who lived in the time of M. Antoninus, and the few remaining fragments of whose works have been edited by Fabricius in his Bibliotheca Græca, Lib. i. cap. 3. ed. 2da. Edit. Harles, Lib. XIII. But there is nothing in these fragments resembling these verses, nor in the fragments of a Latin poet of the same name contained in Maittaire's *Corpus Poetarum Latinorum*, Vol. II.]

that is good, beautiful, or pleasant. For eternal life, or eternal salvation, is nothing else but man's everlasting and alway continuing state, which by means of the best things of all is fully perfect. This state is given us through the beholding or sight, through the fruition, and through the communion or fellowship, which we shall have with the blessed God in the world to come. Hereof is it that St Augustine saith, Lib. xxii. *De Civitate Dei*, cap. 29 : " If I be demanded, what the blessed shall do in this spiritual body, I shall not say that I now see, but that which I believe. Therefore I say, that even in this body they shall see God[2]." Thus also did holy Job hold thereof, and said : " I shall see him to myself, and mine own eyes shall see him, yea, I and none other." Even of this occasion spake St Augustine in the last chapter of this twenty-second book[3], that " the corporal eyes of the body raised up shall execute their office," that is, " they shall see." What he further treated of the beholding of God, it is penned at large in the 112th epistle which he wrote *Ad Paulinam*[4]. Our Lord Jesus saith also in the holy gospel: " This is the eternal life, that they know thee to be the only true God, and whom thou hast sent, Jesus Christ." This knowledge is not only belief and the knowledge of understanding, but also the present beholding and fruition of God, and the fellowship with God, which after this life shall happen unto all faithful believers. For Paul said : " We see now through a glass in a dark speaking, but then face to face." For faith is a stedfast substance of things that we hope for, and as a be-

De Civitate Dei, Lib. xxii. Cap. 29.

Job xix.

Lib. xxii.

Epist. 112. ad Paulin.

John xvii.

1 Cor. xiii.

[2 Cum ex me quæritur, quid acturi sint sancti in illo corpore spiritali, non dico quod jam video, sed dico quod credo. Dico itaque, quod visuri sint Deum in ipso corpore. August. de Civ. Dei, Lib. xxv. cap. 29. Opera, Tom. v. p. 217. A. ed. 1541.]

[3 Augustine, in a long passage immediately following that which he had cited before, goes on to discuss the question,—" In what manner the righteous shall see God ?" and he thus concludes: " Ita Deus erit nobis notus atque conspicuus, ut videatur spiritu a singulis nobis in singulis nobis, videatur ab altero in altero, videatur in seipso, videatur in cœlo novo et in terra nova, atque in omni quæ tunc fuerit creatura; videatur et per corpora in omni corpore, quocunque fuerint spiritalis corporis oculi acie perveniente directi. Ib. p. 217. H.]

[4 August. Opera, Tom. ii. pp. 109-114.]

holding or sight of God; albeit somewhat more dark, and not so evident and clear as shall be that, which, as a reward of faith, shall be given to the faithful in the world to come. "To see face to face," is nothing else but to use, enjoy, and have the fruition of all things presently; also to behold the promise, and perfectly to be partaker thereof. Therefore saith the holy apostle John yet more evidently: "Dearly beloved, we are now the children of God, and yet it doth not appear what we shall be; but we know that when he shall appear, we shall be like him; for we shall see him as he is." With the which words St John will declare three things: namely, that even now in this very present time we are God's children, and therefore also heirs. And though this be a great foredeal, and an excellent jewel, yet the great and unspeakable glory, that in time to come shall be declared in us, hath not yet appeared. "For we," saith he, "shall be like him," namely, our Lord Jesu Christ, who, according to the saying of Paul, "shall alter and change our vile body, that he may make it like unto his own glorious body." Besides this, "even as he is, shall we see him," namely, Christ the Lord; not only as man, but also as very God. Therefore shall we see God as he is, namely, God as the chief and brightest good in whom we have all good things. For Paul saith: "When all things are subdued unto the Son, then shall the Son also be subject unto him who unto him hath subdued all things, that God may be all in all." And therefore said he also in the gospel, that "they know thee to be the only true God." Not that Christ is not very God, but that the mystery and the entreating of the Son, our mediator and reconciler, shall after the judgment be no more so in heaven, as it hath been afore upon earth; but the only God in the holy Trinity shall be of all good the full perfect sufficiency to all faithful. For all that we can wish, think, and desire, shall only God give and be in all things.

And that is also the meaning and understanding of Paul, when he saith, "God shall be all in all." And hereunto serveth now the goodly sentence of St Augustine, who saith thus: "God shall be the end of all our longing and desire; him shall we perpetually see; him shall we love without tediousness and grief; and him shall we praise without ceasing[1]." For tediousness and grief runneth customably with saturation or fulness. As for us, we shall with the beholding of God be filled to the bodily satisfying; which filling shall be as little tedious or grievous, as we are grieved at the waters and rivers that still run into the sea, and yet out of the ground of the earth spring forth again. For the same cometh to pass without all men's tediousness, yea, rather with great joy and commodity, seeing they water and moisture all things, and make them fruitful. And hereunto serve now those testimonies of the scripture. The prophet David saith: "In thy presence is the fulness of joy, and at thy right hand there is pleasure for evermore:" that is, in the beholding of thee is and consisteth all joy, and in heaven shall everlasting pleasure be. Item: "In thy righteousness shall I behold thy face; and when I awake, with thy righteousness shall I be satisfied." Unto the Lord saith also the holy apostle Philip: "Lord, shew us the Father, and it sufficeth us." Therefore the poet Marcellus[2] spake very christianly and well in these his verses: [Psalm xvi.] [Psalm xvii.]

Hereof hath God	And what in the air
His name truly,	Is beautiful,
Because the highest	That may delight,
Good is he.	And be fruitful;
For where he is,	There is in all that
There is present	Number not one,
Much honour and	Which is not seen
Glory excellent.	At all season
And therefore every	Within the circle
Pleasant thing,	Of heaven, I wis,
That water and earth	Where the highest
Doth here forth bring;	Father's dwelling is.

The blessed also and elect shall, in the heavenly and eternal country, with continual praise incessantly laud and

[[1] Sic enim et illud recte intelligitur, quod ait apostolus, Ut Deus sit omnia in omnibus. Ipse finis erit omnium desideriorum nostrorum, qui sine fine videbitur, sine fastidio amabitur, sine fatigatione laudabitur. August. de Civ. Dei, Lib. xxii. cap. 3. Opera, Tom. v. p. 218. L. ed. 1541.]

[[2] Compare p. 214, and the note on that passage.]

magnify the name of God. For what St John in his Revelation thought to signify and shew, thus he said: "I heard the voice of many angels which were about the throne, and about the beasts, and the elders. And I heard many thousands that sung a new song, saying, Worthy is the Lamb that was killed to receive power, and riches, wisdom and strength, honour, glory, and blessing, &c." Moreover, the same eternal life shall be altogether free, and discharged from all heaviness, sickness, and temptations, whereas temporal joy, rest, and welfare of men is mixed with sorrow; as also the holy apostle John doth witness: "I John," saith he, "saw that holy city new Jerusalem coming down from God out of heaven, prepared as a bride garnished for her husband. And I heard a great voice out of heaven, saying, Behold, the tabernacle of God is with men, and he will dwell with them, and they shall be his people, and God himself shall be with them, and shall be their God. And God shall wipe away all tears from their eyes, and there shall be no more death, neither sorrow, neither crying, neither shall there be any more pain; for the old things are gone. And he that sat upon the seat said, Behold, I make all things new: and he said unto me, Write, for these words are faithful and true." And hereunto in manner serveth all that followeth after in the 21st chapter to the end of the book.

_{Rev. v. xiv.}

CHAPTER XXXII.

THE SOULS DEPARTED WOT NOT WHAT THEY DO THAT ARE ALIVE, THEREBY ANY THING TO BE DISQUIETED.

THEREFORE did holy Augustine also teach, that the souls of those that are departed wot not what they do which are alive. Yet will I recite his words. Thus saith Augustine: "If the souls of those that are departed were among the doings of such as are alive, they should, when we see them in sleep, talk with us and them. I will not speak of others at all, lest my good and faithful mother, that by water and land followed me so far to be with me, should now not for-

_{De Cura pro mortuis agenda, cap. 13.}

sake me. For God forbid that he should have made that blessed life more unfriendly or more terrible. God forbid, that when my heart doth any thing press and unquiet me, she should not comfort me her son, whom she yet so entirely loved, that she could never suffer or see me heavy. Undoubtedly it must needs be true that the holy psalmist saith: 'My father and my mother have forsaken me; but the Lord hath taken the care to keep me.' If our fathers now and mothers have forsaken us, how can they be then in our cares and doings? and if father and mother do nothing at all in our business, how can we then think that the other dead meddle ought with us, or know what we do or suffer? The prophet Isaiah saith: 'Thou, O God, art our Father; for Abraham wotteth not of us, and Israel knoweth us not.' Seeing then that such honourable patriarchs wist not what was done concerning their people, which came of themselves, to whom yet, as to God's faithful believers, the same people was promised out of their own stock; how can then the dead open themselves the door, to know and further the doings and not doings of them that are alive? And how shall we be able to say, that they which are dead were helped and eased afore the evil came that followed upon their death, when they after death feel all the calamity and misery of man's life that here happeneth unto us? Or be we in error that speak such things, and count them to be in rest; or doth he err, that maketh the unquiet way of the living so careful and full of cumbrance? I pray thee, what great benefit is it then, that our Lord God promised the virtuous king Josiah, namely, that he should die, because he should not see the great misery, which God threatened unto all the land and people of Israel? The words of the Lord unto Josiah are these: 'Thus saith the Lord God of Israel, Seeing that by reason of my words which thou hast heard, thy heart hath melted, and thou hast humbled thyself before the Lord, when thou heardest what I had threatened unto this place, and to the inhabitants thereof, namely how they shall be destroyed, destitute, and accursed; and thou thereupon hast rent thy garment, and wept before my sight; behold, I have heard thee, saith the Lord God of hosts, the plague shall not touch thee. Behold, I will gather thee unto thy fathers, and into thy grave shalt thou be laid in

peace, and thine eyes shall not see all the plagues that I will bring upon this land, and upon those that dwell therein.' Lo, this king, standing in awe at the threatening of God, did weep and rend his clothes, and through death that came aforehand was he in safety from all misery to come. For he must afore depart in peace and take rest, lest he should see the great calamity. Therefore the souls of those that are departed must needs be in such a place, where they see not all which is done and happeneth in the life of men[1]."
All this have we taken and written out of the 13th chapter

[[1] Si rebus viventium interessent animæ mortuorum, et ipsæ nos, quando eas videmus, alloquerentur in somniis, ut de aliis taceam, meipsum pia mater nulla nocte desereret, quæ terra marique secuta est, ut mecum viveret. Absit enim, ut facta sit vita meliore crudelis usque adeo, ut quando aliquid angit cor meum, nec tristem filium consoletur, quem dilexit unice, quem nunquam voluit mœstum videre. Sed profecto quod sacer psalmus personat, verum est: *Quoniam pater meus et mater mea dereliquerunt me, Dominus autem assumpsit me.* Si ergo dereliquerunt nos patres nostri, quomodo nostris curis et rebus intersunt? Si autem parentes non intersunt, qui sunt alii mortuorum, qui noverunt quid agamus, quidve patiamur? Esaias propheta dixit: *Tu es enim Pater noster; quia Abraham nos nescivit, et Israel non cognovit nos.* Si tanti patriarchæ quid erga populum ex his procreatum ageretur, ignoraverunt, quibus Deo credentibus populus iste de eorum stirpe promissus est; quomodo mortui vivorum rebus atque actibus cognoscendis adjuvandisque miscentur? Quomodo dicimus eis fuisse consultum, qui obierunt antequam venirent mala, quæ illorum obitum consecuta sunt; si et post mortem sentiunt quæcunque in vitæ humanæ calamitate contingunt? An forte nos errando ista dicimus, et hos putamus quietos, quos inquieta vita vivorum sollicitat? Quid est ergo, quod piissimo regi Josiæ pro magno beneficio promisit Deus, quod esset ante moriturus, ne videret mala, quæ ventura illi loco et populo minabatur? Quæ Dei verba hæc sunt: *Hæc dicit Dominus Israel, Verba mea quæ audisti, et veritus es a facie mea cum audisti, quæ locutus sum de isto loco, et qui commorantur in eo, ut deseratur, et in maledicto sit; et concidisti vestimenta tua, et flevisti coram conspectu meo, et ego audivi, dixit Dominus Deus Sabaoth; non sic (l. idcirco) ego apponam te ad patres tuos, et apponeris cum pace; et non videbunt oculi tui omnia mala, quæ ego induco in locum hunc, et qui commorantur in eo.* Territus iste Dei comminationibus fleverat, et sua vestimenta consciderat; et fit omnium malorum futurorum de properatura morte securus, quod ita requieturus esset in pace, ut illa omnia non videret. Ibi ergo sunt spiritus defunctorum, ubi non vident quæcumque aguntur aut eveniunt in ista vita hominibus. August. De Cura pro mortuis agenda. c. 13. Opera, Tom. IV. p. 215, L. M. et 216, A. ed. 1541.]

of Augustine's book, *De cura pro mortuis agenda*. If the souls now in everlasting salvation have a perfect rest, yea, such a rest as their body which they have put off hath not received again; and seeing that they are yet alive, whom they specially loved, while they were with them in body; how much more perfect joy shall they then first have and possess, when their bodies shall come again, and when they shall see that all their brethren, whom they in this life had loved so entirely afore, are together in honour and glory, when now the time of frailty hath ceased, and when in the eternal time there can now no cause of heaviness and grief be thought upon, nor found any more at all! Therefore the glory and joy, which the mercy of God shall after the last judgment give unto men that are made whole again of body and soul, shall be without sorrow, and in all points perfect. And like as the ungodly and unbelievers shall be gathered together with the devil and all his companions; so shall also the righteous and elect have the joyful fruition of the company and fellowship of their head Jesus Christ, and of his members, that is, of all faithful believers.

CHAPTER XXXIII.

THE FAITHFUL SHALL KNOW ONE ANOTHER IN HEAVEN.

THEN also shall the blessed know one another again, having joy together, and rejoicing in the obtained health. For if there should be no knowledge, to what end then should the bodies rise again; or what fruit and profit should the resurrection have; or how might the sentence of Daniel [Daniel xii.] the prophet be verified, when he saith, "They that have instructed and taught others unto godliness, shall shine, and be as light as the stars in the firmament?"

When the Lord was risen again from death, and had taken upon him his glorified body, the apostles knew him; yea, so perfectly and thoroughly well knew they him, that, as St John witnesseth, "none durst say, Who art thou? for [John xxi.] they all knew that it was the Lord." I pass over that the Lord spake in the gospel, saying, "When the Son of man [Luke xxii.]

shall sit upon the seat of his majesty, then shall ye also sit upon twelve seats, and judge the twelve tribes of Israel." For if they that rise again shall not know one another, how shall then the apostles judge and give sentence upon those, to whom they preached here in their lifetime? Note, that the apostles shall not judge in the room and place of their Lord, to whom only is given all power to judge: but this understanding it hath, that the apostles do then judge, when they are there at the judicial court, as witnesses of the righteous judgment of God, with the which he condemneth the unbelievers. For whereas the unbelievers would not give credence to the apostles, that is to say, their preachers, but cried out upon them, as upon ungodly heretics; when they now shall see those present with the Judge of all men, they shall immediately be overcome by the apostles, and have witness in themselves, that they shall be and are justly condemned.

And for this matter read the 4th and 5th chapters of the Book of Wisdom; which serveth very well to this purpose. And seeing it is manifest, that in the life to come even the wicked shall know the good, how much more then shall one good person know another, and one faithful another! In the transfiguration of the Lord upon the mount appeared Moses and Elias, and were known of the three disciples of the Lord; yea, they knew the Lord himself, though he was now transfigured. Hereunto serveth it also that Paul saith: "Ye are come to the city of the living God, to the celestial Jerusalem, and to an innumerable multitude of angels, and to the congregation of the firstborn sons which are written in heaven, and to the spirits of the perfect righteous," &c. Besides this, we have for us the uniform and universal opinion of all faithful, which also witnesseth, that in the life to come the blessed shall know one another. For when we talk of death and of the state and ease of the life to come, we say, though now we must depart asunder, yet shall we see one another again in the eternal country.

<small>Heb. xii.</small>

Socrates also, the right famous and most excellent among all the wise men of the heathen, marked such a like thing, and saw it as in a dream, when, as Cicero witnesseth of him, he was of death condemned of the judges or council, and now should drink the poison. For he said: "O how much better

<small>In Tuscul. Quæst.[i. 41.]</small>

and more blessed is it to go unto them, that well and uprightly lived here in time, than to remain here in this life upon earth! O how dear and worthy a thing is it, that I may talk with Orpheus, Musæus, Homerus, Hesiodus, with those excellent men! Verily, I would not only die once, but many and sundry times also, if it were possible, to obtain the same," &c. After this sort, like as in a dream, did the good philosopher imagine in himself joys vain and of none effect.

But we promise to ourselves true assured joy, in that we hope and know, that in the eternal and everduring country, after the resurrection of the dead, we shall see Adam, our first father; Noah, the dearly beloved friend of God; Abraham, to whom God made special great promises; Moses, the most gentle-hearted man, and one that had greatest experience of all the mysteries of God; Samuel, the friendly and loving prophet; David, the king and prophet, who was God's elect, according to his own will and desire; Josiah, the most godly and best among all the kings of Judah; and also John the Baptist, holier than whom there was none born of woman; and with all these the holy virgin Mary, the mother of God, and highly replenished with grace among all women: item, Peter, John, James, chiefest of the apostles, with the other disciples of Christ; Paul, the famous teacher of the heathen, and all the holy congregation of the patriarchs, prophets, apostles, martyrs, and faithful believers. <small>Adam. Noah. Abraham. Moses. Samuel. David. Josiah. John the Baptist. Mary. Peter. John. James. Paul.</small>

As for our glorified and pure understanding and memory, now endued with immortality, the multitude and infinite number of the blessed in our said native country shall neither grieve nor entangle the same.

From the beginning of the creation there was in Adam a wonderful and excellent efficacy of understanding and remembrance; forasmuch as unto all things and to every one in especial, whatsoever was within the whole compass of the world created, yea, in paradise also, he gave their names, and knew every one. A much more excellent, more pure, and more clear understanding shall God give to the raised up and glorified bodies, so that they shall not lack nor be destitute of any thing at all. And whereas the blessed shall rejoice and have joy together one with another;

yet shall their delight be in the only God, who shall be all in all.

Of these everlasting and heavenly things more and further to write I have not at this present. Howbeit there shall be graciously given us things far greater, much more glorious, more joyful, and more divine, than we can comprehend; namely, salvation, as it is in itself, in that day when we, after the overcoming and treading down of death through our Lord Jesus Christ, shall be carried up and taken to heaven into eternal joy and salvation. Touching the which I have hitherto written, not according to the majesty and worthiness thereof, but after my small ability in most humble wise. God the Father of all mercy, through his dear Son our Lord and Redeemer Jesus Christ, vouchsafe graciously to take us poor sinners up to his glory, and after the joyful resurrection of our body, that we long for, to give and shew us the unoutspeakable joy, which he hath prepared for all faithful believers; that we, ever living and having joy in him, may praise him for ever and ever, that is from eternity to eternity! Amen.

WITH CHRIST EVEN IN DEATH IS LIFE.

The Table

THE CONTENTS OF THE FIRST PART

I.	The Author's purpose	17
II.	The Lord rose with his body	18
III.	Appearings of the body raised up	20
IV.	Christ rose not a spirit, but a true body	21
V.	The fruit of Christ's resurrection.	23
VI.	The true ascension of the Lord's real body, and the place that he went to he in	25
VII.	The divers significations of this word *heaven*	28
VIII.	What God's right hand is, and whereto it is referred.	30
IX.	What it is to sit at the right hand of God; how Christ sitteth there, and what he doeth.	31
X.	Christ, as man sitting at God's right hand, is circumscribed of place	33
XI.	Manner of sitting at the right hand of God, by the which Christ is every where.	38
XII.	The fruit of the corporal ascension of Christ, both in that he doth for us, and in that we learn thereby	40

THE CONTENTS OF THE SECOND PART

XIII.	Of the true resurrection of our flesh	43
XIV.	Our flesh or body itself shall rise again, though it be hard to believe, and what the flesh or body is	44
XV.	The manner how the bodies shall rise again, and the kind that they shall be of....	52
XVI.	That Paul spake rightly of a glorified body, and what a glorified body is, and what a natural	54

XVII.	The case of our members in the body's resurrection, and of their functions	57
XVIII.	The divers errors that sprung about the article of the body's resurrection	59
XIX.	The errors of Origen concerning the resurrection confuted by Jerome	62
XX.	St Jerome's opinion of the resurrection	66
XXI.	St Augustine's mind of the same.	68
XXII.	Aurelius Prudentius of the same.	71
XXIII.	The bodies of unbelievers shall verily rise again	73

THE CONTENTS OF THE THIRD PART

XXIV.	The death and damnation of the ungodly	77
XXV.	That there is an eternal damnation, and the soul is passible	78
XXVI.	The unbelievers' bodies being raised are passible.	80
XXVII.	The pains of hell, matter for continuance of them, with the space of the place and kinds of the punishments	81
XXVIII.	The refutation of such as denied the pain of the damned - to be eternal.	84
XXIX.	That there is an eternal life and salvation.	87
XXX.	Where the place of the faithful is	88
XXXI.	How their salvation shall be	89
XXXII.	The dead wot not what the quick do	94
XXXIII.	The faithful shall know one another in heaven.	97

Appendix

Heaven, Sheol, and Gehenna: What Happened to Heaven and Hell?

by R. Magnusson Davis, B.A., LL.B.
Founder, New Matthew Bible Project

Heaven, Sheol, and Gehenna: What Happened to Heaven and Hell?
Copyright © 2020 by Ruth Magnusson (Davis)

All rights reserved. This work may not be reproduced in whole or in part in any form (beyond such copying as is permitted by applicable law, and except for reviewers for the public press and excerpts of 200 words or less with credit to the author and citation of this book), without written permission from the publisher.
Contact at www.baruchhousepublishing.com.

Scripture quotations are from The October Testament, the New Testament of the New Matthew Bible (NMB), and the 1537/1549 Matthew Bible (MB). Quotations from other Bible versions are for the purposes of comment, criticism, and education only.

Contents of Appendix

Preface ... 109

PART ONE ... 111

The hope of the faithful, and the grave from which we are dug. The traditional (patristic and early Reformation) understanding of what the Bibles teaches about heaven and hell, as drawn from *The Hope of the Faithful* by Myles Coverdale and Otho Wermullerus.

PART TWO ... 129

The "Larger Hope" and lesser grave taught in the 1894 Revised Version of the Bible. The assault on the doctrine of eternal retribution and re-definition of the Hebrew word *sheol* by the scholars who made and promoted the Revised Version.

PART THREE ... 159

The treatment of *sheol* in the 1537 Matthew Bible, and what can be learned from John Rogers' learned definitions. Comparing the different treatments of the Geneva Bible, Revised Version, and modern Bibles. The problems with the modern translations.

Preface

MYLES COVERDALE WAS one of the co-authors of the 1537 Matthew Bible (MB), together with William Tyndale and John Rogers, during the Reformation of the early 16th century. As seen in the preface to *The Hope of the Faithful*, Coverdale complained at that time that, "The devil has sore assaulted the Church by men of great authority and learning [who deny] there is an eternal life and damnation." To refute these men, he translated *The Hope* from the German work of Otho Wermullerus. It was a masterful review of biblical teaching about heaven and hell, and I will rely on it now in this essay, to refute a modern assault on orthodox doctrine – one which has again been mounted by men of great authority and learning. Coverdale and Wermullerus would be pleased to see their work used this way, and I am grateful to them for giving it to us.

There is today a great deal of uncertainty and disagreement concerning what the Bible says about hell. Some people believe the Old Testament did not say or teach anything about it. This is due in part to the trend in modern Bibles to put "Sheol" where earlier versions had "hell" in the Old Testament. Some people question how Sheol, which they believe to be the abode of all departed spirits, differs from hell, where only the wicked go. A friend recently commented to me, "I have heard people use 'Sheol' as a way of lessening the justice of judgement, softening it." People also wonder if hell is a real place, or if it will not come into existence until after the judgement.

Certain modern scholars have created this confusion. Since the late 19th century, they have obscured the orthodox doctrine by new Bible translations, and by popular reference works which re-define the Hebrew word *sheol* and the Greek *hades*, as will be shown. They have orchestrated and led a massive assault on the truth. However, truth can refute and expose their falsehood. The truth was clearly laid out in *The Hope of the Faithful*, as well as in John Rogers' learned notes and expositions in the 1537 Matthew Bible, which we will also see.

Finally, when comparing translations, I do not comment on them as translations per se, but consider their meaning and import. I am not qualified to discuss questions of Hebrew or Greek, and in any case, source language grammatical and interpretive arguments are inconclusive; the very different translations themselves reveal the possible scope for disagreement, debate, and reinterpretation. Also, for the reasons we will see, it cannot help to refer to modern Hebrew or Greek texts. Furthermore, the faith, calling, and doctrine of a translator are just as important as his or her linguistic expertise. It is sufficient to compare translations and make a judgement informed by an understanding of other relevant factors, of which there are many.

Ruth Magnusson Davis

Part One

The hope of the faithful and the grave from which we are dug. Patristic and early Reformation doctrine.

In *The Hope of the Faithful,* Otho Wermullerus did not soften the teachings of hell. I wish to begin by saying that my purpose in reviewing all the unhappy teachings here is not to dwell on hell's misery, from which I take no pleasure at all. However, if these things are true, it is right and even necessary to speak them. Further, they show how great is our salvation in the Lord. The prophet Isaiah cried, "Hearken unto me, ye that hold of righteousness, ye that seek the Lord! Take heed unto the stone from which ye are hewn, and the grave from which ye are dug" (Isa. 51:1, lightly updated). To take heed to the darkness and deepness of the grave from which we are dug is to fall on our faces before the Lord in fear, awe, and gratitude.

There is an eternal hell

Chapter XXVIII (28) of *The Hope of the Faithful* is entitled "The refutation of them that denied the punishment of the ungodly to be eternal." Selected excerpts follow below. (The obsolete English in all quotations from this and other chapters in *The Hope* will be updated for clarity's sake.) Drawing first on the Old Testament,

Wermullerus wrote:

> St. Augustine says in the last book of *The City of God*, that some people have been so merciful, that they dare promise grace, deliverance, and life even to those that are damned and adjudged to eternal death. The same says also St. Jerome, in his writing upon the last chapter of Isaiah. But no one ought to be swayed by such a foolish and erroneous opinion of certain unbelievers, which faithful men have always rejected. For [the Scriptures] speak simply and plainly, that the punishment and damnation of the ungodly or unbelievers is everlasting; and not only of long continuance, as some expound it, but so great, that it cannot be expressed, and so perpetual, that it is without end....
>
> Isaiah says, "Thy rivers shall become resin, and the dust brimstone, the earth burning pitch, not able to be quenched day or night. The smoke shall eternally go up; from generation to generation shall there be a destruction; neither shall any man be able to walk there in everlasting eternity." The prophet doubtless speaks of hell, minding with many words to declare that the punishment and pain of hell is eternal and without end. For first he says, "Day and night it shall not be quenched." Then he says further, "The smoke shall go up forevermore." Also, yet more plainly, "From generation to generation there shall be a destruction"; namely, a dwelling in which there is nothing but pain and undoing. And at the end he adds, "Neither shall anyone be able to walk there in the everlasting eternity," which is such a manner of speech that scarcely anything could more distinctly, evidently, and plainly express the eternity. For what else is the everlasting eternity, but a time without end? But

THE TRADITIONAL DOCTRINE OF ETERNAL RETRIBUTION

> [not] to be able to dwell or walk there means not that no one shall dwell in hell, but that it is a loathsome and horrible place, where everyone desires neither to dwell nor walk. (*Hope,* Ch. XXVIII)

Wermullerus explained that the righteous and unrighteous have separate eternal destinies:

> In the holy prophet Daniel it is written thus: "They [the righteous] who have instructed the multitude unto godliness shall shine as the stars *in seculum et in perpetuum,* forever and ever." Now lest by this word *seculum* anyone should understand a long season, as a hundred, or a thousand, or ten thousand years, he adds immediately *in perpetuum*; that is, to the eternity, or forevermore.
>
> And as eternity is appointed for the righteous, so is there an everlasting eternity ordained for the wicked. For the Lord says plainly, "they that have done good shall come forth to the resurrection of life, and they that have done evil to the resurrection of judgement" [Joh. 5]. Note here the manner of speech: "to the resurrection of life, and to the resurrection of judgement." Now I have shown before that this saying, "to rise up unto the resurrection of judgement," is as much as to rise to a continual and still-remaining state, in which the raised-up bodies endure perpetually in torment.
>
> We find also the like in the same Gospel of John, that the Lord says, "Whoever believes on the Son has eternal life, but he who believes not the Son shall not see life, but the wrath of God abides on him" [Joh. 3:36]. Lo, what could be more evidently and pithily spoken? "He shall not see life," says the Lord. Note: "the wrath of God remains upon

him." If he shall not see life, how shall he then, as those men say, be preserved or saved? Note: if "the wrath of God abides upon him," then surely the vengeance, which is the pain and punishment, shall not be taken away from him. And note that he says the wrath of God abides, yea, abides [*remains*] on him – as if he would say, the punishment hangs upon him, sticks fast, moves not away, alters not, but works in the unbelievers without ceasing, forevermore.

The Lord says, "All sins shall be forgiven the children of men, and also the blasphemies wherewith they blaspheme, but whoever blasphemes the Holy Spirit has no forgiveness forevermore, but is liable to eternal judgement" [Mk. 3:29]. "Forevermore," he says, "has he no remission." And to this he adds, "He is in danger of eternal judgement"; that is, he shall be punished with everlasting, continual punishment. The Lord says moreover in the same Evangelist, "Better it is for thee to enter into life halt or lame, than, having two feet, to be cast into hell fire, the fire that never quenches, where their worm dies not and their fire goes not out [Mk. 9:45-6]." He repeats here once again, "the fire never quenches," and adds thereto that "the worm never dies." Therefore, as the bodies continue forever, so endures their worm also perpetually. For the worm lives and is sustained only by the body or carrion.

St. John also says in his Revelation, "If any man worship the beast and his image, and receive his mark in his forehead, or in his hand, the same shall drink the wine of the wrath of God, which is poured in the cup of his wrath; and he shall be punished in fire and brimstone before the holy angels and before the Lamb. And the smoke of their torment ascends up forevermore, and they have no rest, day or night, etc." [Rev. 14]. And the like is repeated in the 20th chapter. (Ch. XXVIII)

And so there is an eternal hell. But what more can we or should we know? Where is it, and when and how do people go there? The same questions may be asked about heaven. Further, will things change after the general resurrection and final judgement, and if so, how?

About heaven and hell: Summary of the teaching

Wermullerus answered most questions a person might have, with many references to the Old and New Testaments. He also cautioned readers against being "curious" about the things that are hidden from us. (Perhaps the fate of unbaptized infants is one such thing.) I will summarize my understanding of the main points here, followed by more excerpts from his book as translated by Coverdale:

(1) Every human being is both body and spirit (or soul, as Wermullerus says).

(2) After death, the natural bodies of all people, believers and unbelievers alike, go to their grave, whether in the earth or the sea. This is the common death.

(3) After death, the souls, or spirits, of the unrighteous go to a place represented in Scripture as being down below the earth. All people who have died without a saving faith, including in Old Testament times, are there. Until the advent of the Revised Version of the Bible, this place was usually called "hell" or "the pit," and sometimes the "lower habitations," "the deep," etc. It is

depicted as having different depths (which, it seems, represent different degrees of punishment, suffering, or evil). In hell, the souls of the unjust and the unsaved await the second coming of the Lord and final judgement. In this interim state, they are conscious, awake, and aware of suffering.

(4) However, after death the souls of believers – those who are saved and redeemed in Christ – go up to heaven to be with the Lord, there to await his return to the earth. Those who have died in the faith in all ages, including Old Testament times, are in heaven. In this interim state, they are conscious of pleasure and peace.[1]

(5) At the second coming of the Lord, the spirits or souls of all the dead, both the unsaved and the saved, will be reunited with their bodies. In a tremendous feat of divine power, their bodies will be raised from their graves and joined with their disembodied spirits.

(6) All the newly raised dead, together with all who are living when the Lord returns, will then appear before the Great White Throne for a swift judgement. At this final judgement, they will be sentenced to receive in their own flesh the due recompense for the things that they did while they were in their bodies (2Co. 5:10), whether good or evil. Since the body is used by man as an instrument of both good and evil, it must also be judged. Woe then to the evil, both great and small.

(7) At the final judgement, which Wermullerus refers to as "doomsday," the unjust shall be turned back, both body and soul, into hell, to live out their eternal sentence. The reward or suffering of the unjust will be in accordance with the nature and extent of their evil. Further, they will be forever in the company

of the demons and foul spirits.² For the devil and his evil angels will also, at the judgement, be cast out of the earth, and will take up their habitation beneath.

(8) Those who are redeemed and forgiven in Christ Jesus will, after the judgement, inhabit the new heavens and earth in glorified bodies, in a world purified of every injurious thing. They will be joyous in God's presence, and in the presence of the good and holy angels, each other, and the Lord himself. They will be rewarded according to their labours and virtues in this life, as the Scripture says (1Co. 3:8, Ac. 24:16).

Hell and heaven are real places, though many secrets are hid from us

Hell is a sure and certain place. Wermullerus writes:

> Touching the place of punishment, or where the souls with their bodies shall be tormented, the Scripture says simply and plainly that the unbelievers go down into hell. From this it is easy to perceive that hell is under us in the earth. Notwithstanding, to go about to describe, to show and compare precisely the place and the room where it lies, and to print it, does not truly become us, but is a foolish presumption. The testimonies of the Scripture are simple and plain. For the prophet David says, "Let death fall suddenly upon them, and let them go down quick into hell; for wickedness is in their houses and private chambers."... In Luke, the hell is placed beneath, downwards ... Isaiah also speaks of hell, and says, "the Lord has set hell in the deep, and made it wide." (Ch. XXVI)

Heaven is also a sure and certain place. Wermullerus begins this discussion by explaining that the Scripture uses the word "heaven" in various ways, to indicate outer space, the air, or the skies, depending on the context. However, there is a fourth sense:

> Though God is infinite and cannot be compassed about with any place, as the most wise Solomon said ... yet the Scripture calls the heaven that is above us a dwelling of God, which dwelling is ordained for all faithful and virtuous believers, and is named "the heaven." Paul witnesses to this, saying, "We know that if our earthly place of this dwelling were destroyed, we have a building of God, a habitation not made with hands, but eternal in heaven." There heaven is taken for the kingdom of God, for the kingdom of the Father, or joy and eternal life, which is peace and rest. The heaven, I say, is a seat and dwelling of the faithful, or blessed believers; a determinate place also, into which the Lord Jesus was received when he was taken up into the heaven.
>
> And this does the Scripture plainly declare to us; namely, that above us there is a certain determinate place prepared for us. For Luke says, "He was received upon high, and a cloud took him up away out of their sight." Note, "And while they looked steadfastly up towards heaven, the Angels said, this same Jesus, who is taken away from you into heaven, shall so come even as you have seen him go into heaven." Who is so ignorant now, that he does not know where heaven is, or the clouds, or into which heaven the apostles looked so steadfastly? ... Paul also says in another place, "If you are risen again with Christ, then seek those things which are above, where Christ sits at the right hand

of God." And therefore the Lord Jesus has gone up into the heaven that is above us; namely, into that sure certain place that is prepared for the blessed. (Ch. VII)

However, Wermullerus said that, as it is with hell, so it is with heaven: it behoves us not to be overmuch "curious" about the secret things, which have yet to be revealed (156). Rogers wrote to this effect in a note in the 1537 Matthew Bible concerning Luke's parable of poor Lazarus, whom the Lord described as being in Abraham's bosom after he died:

> **Rogers' note on Luke 16:22, NMB:** By Abraham's bosom some understand the faith of Abraham. Some also understand it of the place where the elect and chosen, who follow the faith of Abraham, rest after their death. But where that place is (because the Scripture does not expressly determine it,) we cannot tell, and therefore no man may be so bold as to define it.

However, though much remains a mystery, it is evident that the place of the elect and chosen is a separate place, and one to which the unjust cannot go. That was the Lord's teaching on the parable, when he said that there was a great chasm between Lazarus and the rich man.

The interim state of the soul, believers and unbelievers

It remains to consider more closely the condition of departed spirits until the resurrection. Wermullerus taught that they are conscious and passible; that is, they are able to experience sensation and emotion. To prove this, he drew upon the Lazarus parable:

> There are some who think that, seeing the soul is a spirit, it cannot, neither may suffer; yea, that it is not subject to any passion [*sensation*] at all. Therefore, against such teachers I will set now the soul of the luxurious rich man in the gospel, who expressly and plainly says, "O send Lazarus, that he may dip the tongue of his finger in water, and cool my tongue; for I am tormented in this flame." Lo, the rich man's soul is tormented in fire. On this it follows that the souls are passible, and subject to suffer. And all this is shown to us by the Lord as a parable, yet it is done for this intent, even to describe and show to us the state and case of the souls that are separated from their bodies. (Ch. XXV)

Ezekiel testified in the Old Testament about the fate of Pharaoh and the cruel Egyptians, who, upon their deaths, would descend to "the lower habitations" to join those already there. This passage is one of the clearest to describe the nature of hell, and to show that it is a real place under the earth, where the "uncircumcised" (unbelievers) go, and where they mourn:

> **Ezekiel 31:15-18, MB** Thus says the Lord God: In the day when he goeth down to the grave, I will cause a lamentation to be made. I will cover the deep upon him ... I will make the heathen shake at the sound of his fall, when I cast him down to hell, with them that descend into the pit. ... [they] shall mourn with him also in the lower habitations: for they shall go down to hell with him, unto them that be slain with the sword ... Yet art thou cast down under the earth (among the trees of Eden) where thou must lie among uncircumcised, with them that be slain with the sword.

As to believers, Wermullerus gave the example of Steven to show that after death their spirits are received immediately into heaven, where they are joyful:

> The heaven, into which Christ ascended with his true body, is even the same place and rest that faithful believers are taken up into. And into the same heaven Steven desired to be received when he lifted up his eyes into heaven and saw Jesus standing at the right hand of the father, to whom he committed his soul and said, "O Lord Jesus, receive my spirit." (Ch. XXX) ... If the souls now in everlasting salvation have a perfect rest – yea, such a rest as their body, which they have put off, has not received back again, and seeing that they are yet alive ... how much more perfect joy shall they then first have and possess when their bodies shall come back again, and when they shall see that all their brethren, whom they in this life had loved so entirely before, are together in honour and glory, when now the time of frailty has ceased, and when in the eternal time there can now be no cause of heaviness and grief. (Ch. XXXII)

Of the end of the age and of this world

Of the momentous things that will occur at the end of the age, Wermullerus wrote:

> But to the intent that this may yet be more plainly understood, I will now tell how our bodies shall rise, and of what nature and kind they shall be in the resurrection. At the end of the world the Lord shall come with great majesty and judgement, and shall declare and show himself in and with a right true, real body. Hither also too shall he be brought,

and shall stand in the clouds of heaven so that all flesh may see him; yea, all men that are upon earth shall behold him, and know him by his glory. In the mean season also shall he send his archangel to blow the trumpet. Then shall all the dead hear, and perceive the voice and power of the Son of God. And so all people who died, from the first Adam, shall immediately arise out of the earth. And all they who live until the last day shall, in the twinkling of an eye, be changed. And thus all people, everyone in his own flesh, shall stand before the judgement seat of our Lord Jesus Christ, and shall wait for the last judgement and sentence of the Lord; which sentence being given, quickly and without delay, he shall call one part to heaven and thrust out the other into hell. (Ch. XV)

As to the resurrected bodies of the believers and unbelievers, Wermullerus said:

When the [believer's] body takes upon it the glorification and immortality, [all infirmities] shall be wholly removed and fall away.... The glorified bodies shall be clear, bright, and shining bodies, even as the body of Christ was in his transfiguration upon the mount of Tabor.... Again, glorification comprehends deliverance; that is, the laying away and clear discharge of all these miseries and sorrows. So that now glorification is called (and so it is in very deed) pureness, perfect strength, immortality, and joy; yea, a sure, quiet, and everlasting life. (Ch. XVI)

But to the intent that no one should doubt touching the resurrection of the flesh of the unbelievers, I will bring forth certain testimonies of holy Scripture that do manifestly

THE TRADITIONAL DOCTRINE OF ETERNAL RETRIBUTION

declare that the unbelievers, or ungodly, shall with their own true bodies rise again. The prophet Isaiah, in the last chapter of his book, says, "They shall go forth and look upon the bodies of them that have vilely behaved themselves against me; for their worms shall not die, neither shall their fire be quenched, and all flesh shall abhor them." With this sentence does the prophet play, after the manner and custom of those who have just gotten the victory, who with great desire, after the battle is one, go out from the city into the field to view and look upon the bodies of those who are slain ... since now Christ also has fought prosperously, overcome his enemies on doomsday, and made them his footstool, the faithful shall go out to see the bodies of the ungodly.

The prophet does for this cause call them bodies, even to show that the bodies raised up from death shall be very true flesh. He continues further also in the sentence and says, "their worms shall not die." For the bodies, or corpses, are full of worms; neither are they anything but worms' meat. Not only the souls, but also the bodies of unbelievers does the Lord destroy. From which it follows that they shall rise again. For if they should not rise again, they could not be tormented and plagued. Neither shall any other body rise again to pain and punishment, but even the same that with its vile works has deserved the plague.... For the body is an instrument or vessel by which something is done, and therefore, in the last judgment of God, the body, according to the divine righteousness, shall not be omitted, neither forgotten at all. (Ch. XXIII)

I confess a personal reluctance to understand "the worm that never dies" literally, as expressed above. But in any case, after the judgement, believers in their glorified bodies will be gathered together to be with the Lord and with each other for eternity. However, the unbelievers will be cast into hell beneath, to spend eternity with the devil and his evil angels:

> The ungodly shall be in the fellowship of most foul spirits, with whom they had their lust in this life. There shall all be full of confusion, loathsome and great torments, and so shall all burn together for eternity. For thus shall the Judge give sentence with plain and expressed words: "Depart from me, ye cursed, into everlasting fire, which is prepared for the devil and his angels." ... And holy Scripture says that the ungodly are given over to the devil to burn perpetually. (Ch. XXVII)

The fruit and blessings of the resurrection of Christ

It is terrible to contemplate these things. But they reveal the greatness of the victory Christ won by his bodily resurrection from death. Wermullerus again:

> Now I will declare the occasion, why I have with such diligence and so earnestly pressed on to this, that Jesus Christ with his true body did truly rise again: that is, how profitable and necessary it is so to believe, and what fruit the true resurrection of Christ does bring and engender unto us. And albeit that hereof, as of a plentiful treasure, much might be spoken, yet will I comprehend it all in a short sum.

> Though we be complete and made perfect through the death of Christ, while the just judgement of God is satisfied, the curse taken away, and the penalty recompensed and paid, yet Peter says that "we are born again through the

THE TRADITIONAL DOCTRINE OF ETERNAL RETRIBUTION

resurrection of Jesus Christ unto a living hope." For just as Christ with his resurrection overcame death, so stands also the triumph and victory of our faith in the resurrection of Christ. Therefore, through his death sin is taken away, and by his resurrection righteousness is brought again. For how could he with his death have delivered us from death, if he himself had been overcome by death? Or, how could he have obtained the victory for us, if he had been destroyed in the battle himself? Therefore, through death is death defeated, and with the resurrection is life to us restored....

And finally, out of the words of the holy apostle Paul, we learn that, through the example of Christ who was raised up, we are not only moved to take upon us a new life, but that we also through the power of Christ are renewed, so that we may lead an innocent and holy life. (Ch. V) ...

Christ also, with his ascension into heaven, thought to show to us his power and might, wherein consists our strength, our power, riches, and triumph against sin, death, world, devil, and hell. For he, ascending up on high, led captivity captive. (Ch. XII)

Thus, briefly re-stated, is the traditional doctrine of heaven and hell, garnered from both the Old and New Testaments and as set forth in *The Hope of the Faithful*.

Four final points

Some final thoughts:

(1) *The second death.* The turning back of unbelievers into hell with their bodies after the judgement is the "second death"

spoken of in Revelation 2, 20, and 21. However, as the Scripture says, the second death will not hurt anyone who had part in the first resurrection. The first resurrection is the new birth, when a person believes on the Son of God; the Lord then, by the power of the Holy Spirit, sets him free from the dominion of the devil, which is the kingdom of death, and raises his soul to eternal life:

> **John 5:24, NMB** Truly truly I say to you, he who hears my words and believes on him who sent me, has everlasting life, and shall not come into damnation, but is escaped from death to life.

> **Revelation 20:6, NMB** Blessed and holy is he who has part in the first resurrection. For on such the second death shall have no power.

(2) *The descent of Christ into hell.* What is the meaning of the confession in the Apostles' Creed, that the Lord "was crucified, died, and was buried; he *descended to hell*; the third day he rose again from the dead and ascended into heaven"? This must be taken at face value. It is no more than a restatement of the Scripture. The prophet Paul wrote, "He ascended up on high, and has led captivity captive, and has given gifts to men. That he ascended, what does it mean but that he also descended first, into the lowest parts of the earth? He who descended is the same also who ascended up, even above all heavens, to fulfil all things" (Eph. 4:8-10. See also Ro. 10:7). The Scripture speaks plainly.

(3) *The spirits in prison.* It is said in 1 Peter that Jesus, after his resurrection, went and preached to the spirits who were in prison. Who were they, and what was the prison? As discussed later, the Hebrew word *bore*, which was often translated "the pit," in one sense referred to a dungeon or pit beneath the earth where

prisoners were held. In this sense it was used in the Old Testament to speak about hell. It is believed that the spirits of certain ancient folk were held in the pit, and Jesus went to preach to them, just as the text says. See the verses and Rogers' note, from the New Matthew Bible:

> **1 Peter 3:18-9** For Christ also suffered once for sins, the just for the unjust, in order to bring us to God; and was killed as concerning the flesh, but was quickened to life in the Spirit. In which Spirit he also went and preached to the spirits who were in prison, who were in time past disobedient, when the longsuffering of God abode exceedingly patiently in the days of Noah, while the ark was being prepared.
>
> **1 Peter 4:6** To this purpose was the gospel [1]preached to the dead: that they should be judged like other men in the flesh, but should live before God in the spirit.
>
> **Note 1:** As certain learned expositors will, that which Peter here calls the preaching of the gospel to the dead, he called in the preceding chapter [3] preaching to the spirits that were in prison. This, they say, means that also to the dead, or the spirits in prison, came the salve or medicine of the gospel and of the glad tidings of Christ's passion, whereby they were released, the power of it being so great that they were brought out of prison to immortality. And because it might be asked how the souls of these blessed ones came forth out of prison – whether in their bodies, or only in the pure substance of the spirit – therefore Peter says that they will be judged like other men in the flesh, that is, when all others shall be judged in the flesh, but they will live before God in the spirit, which signifies that in the meantime, until

the judgement comes, their souls will live and rejoice before God through Christ.

(4) *Sheep fallen into the pit*. Jesus' parable about rescuing a sheep from the pit on the Sabbath day assumes a new meaning when we understand truly about the pit that his sheep have been lifted out of. He it is who rescues the sheep, and now is that Sabbath day.

And thus the deep grave out of which we are dug.

Part Two

The "Larger Hope" and lesser grave of the 1894 Revised Version. The assault on the doctrine of eternal retribution and re-definition of the Hebrew *sheol*.

My 1895 British edition of the Revised Version of the Bible (RV) says, "The revision of the Authorized Version was undertaken in consequence of a Resolution passed by both houses of the Convocation of the Province of Canterbury." The RV New Testament was published in 1881, the Old in 1885, and the Apocrypha in 1894.

In their preface to the New Testament, the scholars of the RV revision committee claimed that their work was a badly needed review and correction of the King James Bible. They condemned the KJV sources and the "character" of that translation:

> **RV, preface to New Testament:** Of the many points of interest connected with the Translation of 1611, two require special notice; first, the Greek Text which it appears to have represented; and secondly, the character of the Translation itself ...
>
> 1. All [the KJV Greek sources] were founded for the most part on manuscripts of late date, few in number, and used with little critical skill. But in those days, it could hardly

have been otherwise. Nearly all the more ancient of the documentary authorities have become known only within the last two centuries ... While therefore it has long been the opinion of all scholars that the commonly received text needed thorough revision, it is but recently that materials have been acquired for executing such a work with even approximate completeness.

2. They [the KJV translators] profess in their Preface to have studiously adopted a variety of expression which would now be deemed hardly consistent with the requirements of faithful translation.... It cannot be doubted that they carried this liberty too far, and that the studied avoidance of uniformity in the rendering of the same words, even when occurring in the same context, is one of the blemishes in their work.[3]

"Little critical skill," "hardly consistent with faithfulness," "blemished," sources that "needed thorough revision," materials not even approximately complete: this was a severe condemnation. It was also false in many respects. The ancient documentary authorities touted by the revisers was a reference to Alexandrian manuscripts used in their New Testament revision, instead of the Received Text (RT) that was used for the KJV. However, it was not true that the Alexandrian manuscripts had "become known only within the last two centuries." They were known in the 16th century when Erasmus first compiled the RT. In fact, Erasmus had a friend who worked in the Vatican library, and he had access to the manuscripts kept there if he had so desired.[4] Further, it is almost blasphemous to say that the RT was inadequate: it was the text God provided to his servants in the Reformation, many of whom sealed their work with their blood at his calling. In other writings some of the RV committee members dared to call the RT "corrupt."[5] These condemnations implied that any New Testament based on the RT – including Tyndale's and Luther's as well as the KJV – was inadequate and "corrupt." Finally, it is a fact that very few of the significant revisions in the RV New Testament – that is, revisions that significantly affected meaning or doctrine – were due to textual variants: the figure has been put at less than 1%.[6] Most were due to variant *interpretations*.[7] Therefore, while the revisers' Greek texts and much-vaunted critical skills were promoted as vital for biblical scholarship, it was all a gigantic red herring and a bundle of evil speaking. In the final analysis, their documentary authorities were helpful for promotion, but hardly relevant to their work. Much more relevant were their private theological opinions.

Fenton Hort's quiet process: Variant interpretations and indirect influences

Not only in the New Testament, but also throughout the Old Testament of the RV, there were many new translations, as well as many new "alternate readings" offered in marginal notes. These changed the meaning of the biblical text. They touched on such matters as the second coming, judgement, and eternal retribution, which we will see here, and also the law, salvation, the New Covenant, the person and work of Jesus, creation, and more (discussed further in *The Story of the Matthew Bible: The Scriptures Then and Now [Story Part 2]*). The new meanings could only have been intentional. The private correspondence of Fenton Hort, a Cambridge professor and a leader of the revision committee, evidences a rejection of, and even a conspiracy against, orthodox doctrine, which he referred to as "traditionalism":

> The errors and prejudices, which we agree in wishing to remove, can surely be more wholesomely and also more effectually reached by individual efforts of an indirect kind than by combined open assault. At present very many orthodox but rational men are being unawares acted on by influences which will assuredly bear good fruit in due time, if the process is allowed to go on quietly; and I cannot help fearing that a premature crisis would frighten back many into the merest traditionalism.[8]

The RV indeed initiated a quiet process of removing traditional doctrine from the Bible. Since its publication, modern versions have taken over many of its new translations, and have also brought its alternate readings from the margins directly into the biblical text, so that over time the meaning of hundreds of verses has been incrementally changed, in ways both great and small. By this means, the influence of the RV has grown over time, even though it was never itself a popular Bible. But no one could have suspected or anticipated its impact from the assurances given by the revisers. Their Old and New Testament prefaces say their guiding principles included:

> 1. To introduce as few alterations as possible into the Text of the Authorized Version consistently [sic] with faithfulness.

> 2. To limit, as far as possible, the expression of such alterations to the language of the Authorized and earlier English Versions.

> 3. We do not contemplate any new translation of the Bible, or any alteration of the language, except where, in the judgement of the most competent scholars, such change is necessary.[9]

These guidelines appear very confining and respectful of orthodoxy. However, given the number of substantive revisions, many items evidently fell within the 3rd principle: the "most competent scholars" judged an alteration, or a note suggesting an alteration, to be necessary – including, though they never said so, doctrinally significant ones. Revisions that affected doctrine were presented as mere "alterations of the language." I will attempt to show that many of these alterations were a covert way, or as Hort said, an indirect way, to remove the teaching of eternal retribution from the Scriptures.

Universalism and the Revised Version

At least some of the leaders and members of the RV revision committee did not believe in eternal retribution. Hort's correspondence, and that of his fellow committee member and Cambridge associate Brooke Westcott, reveal disbelief. They also reveal sympathy for the doctrines of universal salvation and purgatory.[10] Universal salvation, or universalism, is the belief that all people will eventually be saved and that there is no hell: it is heaven without hell. When the RV was published, universalism was being preached as "the Larger Hope." The Roman Catholic doctrine of purgatory holds that, after death, people will only temporarily suffer the consequences of their sins. Hort wrote:

> Finite sin cannot deserve infinite punishment.[11]

> The idea of purgation, of cleansing as by fire, seems to me inseparable from what the Bible teaches us of the Divine chastisements; and, though little is directly said respecting the future state, it seems to me incredible that the Divine

chastisements should in this respect change their character when this visible life is ended.[12]

What Hort fails to understand is that, although the deed passes away in time, the guilt endures, unless forgiven or remitted.

If a person believes there is no eternal retribution, he will understand the second coming of Jesus in a new light. Westcott wrote that when the Lord returns:

> All the tribes of the earth shall mourn over him in penitential sorrow, and not, as [in] the Authorized Version, shall wail because of him, in the present expectation of terrible vengeance.[13]

Westcott suggests that at the second coming, all will repent, or at least will have a new claim on the Lord's mercy. (This is a whole other question; suffice to say that now, in this life, is the time of decision.) Westcott's view was evidently a 3rd principle item, which required an "alteration of the language," and Revelation 1:7 was changed accordingly in the RV New Testament:

Revelation 1:7

KJV He cometh with clouds ... and all kindreds of the earth *shall wail because of him.*

RV He cometh with the clouds ... and all the tribes of the earth *shall mourn over him.*

This was a significant revision, which derogated from the traditional doctrine. And it was only one of many such revisions that had nothing to do with the scholars' much-vaunted documentary authorities.

It is noteworthy that Westcott and Hort held to the concept of progressive revelation; that is, the idea that the biblical covenants or ages have had as a main purpose to advance the knowledge of grace and Christian doctrine, which is one of the tenets of so-called covenant theology. Their ideas were not quite John Calvin's (that Jesus manifested in order to be part of a new external way of teaching the former doctrine,[14] discussed in *Story Part 2*); however, like him they assigned a progressively didactic (instructive) purpose to the biblical covenants. They blended progressive revelation and evolutionary dogma, and treated the second coming and final judgement as the last in a series of divine unveilings that were intended to help man develop in Christian knowledge:

> Hort: There is a present unveiling of him simply as he is, without reference to any special action of his, such as came to St. Paul on his conversion. There are apparently successive unveilings of him, successive Days of the Lord. There is clearly indicated a supreme unveiling, in which glory and judgement are combined.[15]

> Westcott: Do you not understand the meaning of Theological "Development"? It is briefly this, that in an early time some doctrine is proposed in a simple or obscure form, or even but darkly hinted at, which in succeeding ages, as the wants of men's minds grow, grows with them – in fact, that Christianity is always progressive in its principles and doctrines.[16]

The essential problem with the concept of progressive revelation is that it denies the one revelation upon which everything depends: the revelation of Jesus Christ to the human soul. This is a one-time revelation, the experience of being born again, which occurs when a person believes on Christ. Without this revelation, no one can understand the things of the Spirit regardless of how much he progresses in any other kind of knowledge; without this revelation, no one can be saved. Conversely, if, like the thief on the cross, we have only this revelation before we die, it is enough.

Westcott also spiritualized the second coming, describing it as part of a continuing revelation. But worse, another member of the RV revision committee, Vance Smith, completely denied the second coming:

> This idea of the second coming ought now to be passed by as a merely temporary incident of early Christian belief. Like many another error, it has answered its transitory purpose in the providential plan, and may well, at length, be left to rest in peace.[17]

And so, according to this learned doctor, as man becomes wiser, earlier Christian doctrine must be cast aside. And never mind that this is inconsistent with the position the revisers took to promote their Greek manuscripts; viz, that they were from an earlier time, and therefore more reliable. Smith also suggests the early Christians were deceived about the second coming as part of God's "plan" – as if the God of truth deceived his own. But whether the second coming is blasphemously denied like this, or subtly denied by allegorizing it as Hort did, it is false. And Smith's unorthodoxy went even further. He was a Unitarian, and denied the Trinity. The Unitarians in Britain had for years been seeking a revision of the Bible to remove alleged corruptions, such as the Johannine comma in the New Testament, which supports the Trinity. Nonetheless, Westcott and Hort fought for Smith's inclusion on the revision committee;

THE REDEFINITION OF 'SHEOL' IN THE REVISED VERSION

Westcott even threatened to quit if the Convocation ejected him. And Smith was not the only Unitarian on the committee, as will be seen.

These, then, were some of the men who convened to correct the English Bible, and to ensure its faithfulness, language, and character.

New transliterations begin the quiet process of removing "hell" from the Scripture

The RV men mounted a comprehensive attack on the doctrine of eternal retribution. Their first advance was to remove the word "hell" itself from the Scriptures, especially the Old Testament, as much as possible. This was accomplished by the ingenious means of transliterating two of the four words that had previously been translated "hell"; namely, the Hebrew noun *sheol* and the Greek *hades*. Transliteration is not translation. It is the process of representing a foreign word phonetically in the letters of the receptor language. It is generally used only for proper nouns (Israel, Jordan, Satan) and expressions accepted into the language (Amen). However, the RV revisers took the unusual step of transliterating, and even capitalizing, *sheol* and *hades*, to give us "Sheol" and "Hades." The new words were semantically empty in English, so the revisers were now nicely positioned to build a new meaning upon them. Which they did.

In the Old Testament, much turns on the translation and interpretation of the Hebrew noun *sheol*. In their OT preface, the RV revisers obfuscated the reason for the new transliteration, and also avoided saying directly what they believed about eternal retribution:

HEAVEN, SHEOL, AND GEHENNA: WHAT HAPPENED TO HEAVEN AND HELL?

RV preface to the Old Testament: The Hebrew *Sheol*, which signifies the abode of departed spirits, and corresponds to the Greek *Hades*, or the underworld, is variously rendered in the Authorized Version by 'grave,' 'pit,' and 'hell.' Of these renderings 'hell,' if it could be taken in its original sense as used in the Creeds, would be a fairly adequate equivalent for the Hebrew word; but it is so commonly understood of the place of torment that to employ it frequently would lead to inevitable misunderstanding. The Revisers therefore in the historical narratives have left the rendering 'the grave' or 'the pit' in the text, with a marginal note 'Heb. Sheol' to indicate that it does not signify 'the place of burial'; while in the poetical writings they have put most commonly 'Sheol' in the text and 'the grave' in the margin. In Isaiah xiv, however, where 'hell' is used in more of its original sense and is less liable to be misunderstood, and where any change in so familiar a passage which was not distinctly an improvement would be a decided loss, the Revisers have contented themselves with leaving 'hell' in the text, and have connected it with other passages by putting 'Sheol' in the margin.

When I first read this, I was confused. I understood little except that the revisers said *sheol* and *hades* were equivalent, and they wished to avoid suggesting that these words indicated the place of torment. It was not clear why *sheol* did not mean a place of burial but should be defined it in the margins as "grave." The alleged "original sense of hell" in the Creeds – as if it had some lost meaning – was not explained. The revisers appear to wrongly suggest that the Apostles' Creed did not use "hell" in the traditional sense, and to overlook that the Creed of St. Athanasius holds the doctrine of eternal torment to be an essential tenet of the faith.

THE REDEFINITION OF 'SHEOL' IN THE REVISED VERSION

It took me months of research to sort out what the RV revisers really did. I have been obliged to compare all their translations of *sheol* and *bore* (OT), and *hades* and *Gehenna* (NT), with the MB, KJV, and other versions. I have been obliged to review the works of some of the men on the revision committee and the authors they admired. In the end, based on what I now know, I would rewrite the RV preface to explain the true purpose of the transliteration *sheol* as below (tongue-in-cheek, but quite accurate, I believe):

> The Revisers and most competent scholars do not agree with the traditionalists, that the Hebrew *sheol*, which corresponds to the Greek *hades*, indicates a place of retribution and suffering where the wicked go. The place of torment is represented by the term *Gehenna* in the New Testament, and it refers to the place or state to which the devil and evil angels will be consigned after the judgement. *Gehenna* is separate from, or a separate part of, *sheol* (*hades*). There is some uncertainty about whether *Gehenna* has yet been created, or if reprobate men will also go there, or if it is a purgative fire, or even if it is literal or figurative. However, the Revisers agree that the Old Testament said little, if anything, about this place.
>
> The Hebrew *sheol* signifies the place below the earth where the departed spirits of the deceased go. Some of the most competent scholars believe that all persons, including the Old Testament saints, are in *sheol*, and that biblical references to heaven are purely figurative. Others, however, believe heaven is real, and that the deceased saints are in heaven now, later to be joined by virtuous souls from *sheol*. Since there was no consensus, the Revisers accommodated

divers views by defining *sheol* ambiguously as "the abode of the dead." (see Ge. 37:35). Thus they avoided clearly describing it as an interim or permanent abode, and also did not clarify whether it is the abode of *all* the dead or only the unsaved. The Revisers are confident that this obscurity will avoid needless division in the Church. However, they acknowledge that the use of the definite article suggests the dead are not in any other abode, heavenly or otherwise, and the marginal notes upon the historical narratives indicate that all souls, including the patriarch Jacob and King David, are in *sheol* (*hades*). In this regard, they are grateful to their esteemed colleague and member of the American revision committee, Joseph H. Thayer, for his forbearance. They note that, in his *Lexicon of the New Testament,* Dr. Thayer declares the contrary view; namely, that the OT saints are already in heaven.

In order, therefore, to disassociate *sheol* and *hades* from the concept of hell, the Revisers transliterated these words as "Sheol" and "Hades." This alteration of the language helped clear the term "hell" out of the Bible, and enabled the Revisers to develop a new meaning upon the new words. They have contented themselves with leaving the translation "hell" in the OT prophetic books, and also in the NT to translate *Gehenna*.

Thus would a more honest preface read.

The charts on the following page show that the RV revisers reduced the mention of "hell" by about 50% in both the Old and New Testaments. Since then, certain modern translators, who apparently accept that the Hebrew Scriptures did not teach about eternal retribution, have taken the removal to 100% in the Old Testament. The numbers tell the story:

Use of "hell" or "Sheol" in the Old Testament		
Bible version	Hell	Sheol
MB	50	0
GNV	21	0
KJV	31	0
RV	15	15
NKJV	19	13
NIV	0	0*
ESV	0	31
* Used "grave," etc. See Part 3.		

Use of "hell" or "Hades" in the New Testament		
Bible version	Hell	Hades
MB	23	0
GNV	21	0
KJV	23	0
RV	13	10
NKJV	16	11
NIV	13	8
ESV	14	9

HEAVEN, SHEOL, AND GEHENNA: WHAT HAPPENED TO HEAVEN AND HELL?

New notes to re-define "sheol"

So then, the first step in Hort's quiet process was to introduce the new transliterations. The next step was to add a series of marginal notes, which falsely appear merely philological, to develop the desired new meaning and doctrine on the new words. It proceeded thus: hell = Sheol = the grave = the abode of the dead. The notes cross-referenced as follows:

Hell = Sheol	Everywhere "hell" was kept in the RV (which was only in the prophets) there was a note: "Heb. *Sheol*."
Sheol = the grave	Often, where the transliteration "Sheol" was used, the RV had a note: "Or, *the grave*."
Grave = the abode of the dead	Often, where the translation "grave" was used, the RV had a note: "Heb. *Sheol*." Sometimes the note referred the reader to Genesis 37:35, where the note said *Sheol* means "the abode of the dead" (see below).

Thus the (semantically tortured) notes all lead to the definition of *sheol* as "the abode of the dead." And this word "abode" is not benign, but is key to the scholars' re-definition. An "abode" is simply a dwelling place, with no suggestion of fire, pain, or the usual associations with hell. The Oxford English Dictionary (OED) defines it as "a place of ordinary residence."[18] The RV introduced the new definition of *sheol* at the very beginning of the Bible, in Genesis 37. Here the patriarch Jacob had just been told of the apparent death of his son Joseph:

Genesis 37:35

MB He would not be comforted, but said, I will *go down into the grave* unto my son mourning.

RV He refused to be comforted; and he said, For I will *go down to *the grave* to my son mourning.

*RV note: Heb. *Sheol*, the name of the abode of the dead, answering to the Greek Hades, Acts 2:27.

It is enormously significant that the meaning of the RV note is that the patriarch Jacob did not expect to go to heaven when he died, but to join Joseph in a dwelling place beneath the earth, an abode called "the grave," but which is really the place "Sheol." Needless to say, this is contrary to the traditional understanding. Rogers explained in a note on Genesis 42 that the expression "go down to the grave" was used figuratively. It meant that Jacob would join his son *in death*: *sheol* as 'the grave' was a figure of death in a generic sense. In Genesis 42, Jacob did not want his son Benjamin to go down to Egypt with his brothers because he feared some calamity along the way, and he used the same expression again:

Genesis 42:38

MB Some misfortune might happen upon him by the way which ye go. And *so should ye *bring my gray head with sorrow unto the grave*.

*MB note: Bring me to my grave: that is, ye shall bring me to my death, as in Isaiah 38.

RV If mischief befall him by the way in the which ye go, then shall ye *bring down my gray hairs with sorrow to *the grave*.

*RV note: Heb. *Sheol.* See ch. 37:35.

The RV thus re-interpreted the figurative sense of *sheol*, and changed the meaning in Genesis 37 and 42.

This leads to another problem in the RV: *sheol* and *hades* were capitalized. So was *abaddon*, which means "destruction" (rendered "Abaddon"). The problem is that (in English) capitalization indicates a proper noun; in particular, as here, a place name. This limits the meaning to the proper sense, and makes figurative and common senses difficult to derive, as will be seen later. No one would write, "The marriage was Hell," but that is effectively the result when *sheol* is capitalized. Capitalization would be wrong in "The armies left Destruction in their wake." One wonders, who or where is Destruction? Capitalization broke orthographic convention, made it difficult or impossible to understand the full meanings of the words, and turned "*sheol*/a grave/pit/hell" into "Sheol/the abode."

Individual efforts of an indirect kind: New and scholarly reference texts

Another important step in Hort's quiet process to remove traditional doctrine from the Bible was the publication of biblical reference texts – grammars, lexicons, and study guides for popular and academic use – which redefined *sheol* and *hades*. These were powerful "indirect influences." Two of the most effective, considering their popular reach, have been *Strong's Exhaustive Concordance of the Bible* by James Strong, and *Thayer's Greek-English Lexicon of the New Testament* by Joseph H. Thayer. The plot thickens when we learn that both men were part of the RV revision team. Strong was invited by Philip Schaff to join the American revision committee, and he assisted also with the English edition of the RV. Thayer sat on the American committee.

THE REDEFINITION OF 'SHEOL' IN THE REVISED VERSION

Strong's Concordance

Strong published his Concordance in 1890, concurrent with the final preparation of the RV. In his Hebrew and Greek lexicons, he indicated that *sheol* and *hades* are names for one and the same place, and there is no hint that this might be a place of suffering:

> **Strong, Hebrew *sheol* (#7585):** *hades* or the world of the dead (as if a subterranean *retreat*), includ. its accessories and inmates.

> **Strong, Greek *hades* (#86):** the place (state) of departed souls.

When I first realized what Strong had written under *"sheol,"* I was perplexed. Sheol and Hades are a *retreat*? The "inmates" are in a *retreat*? Words matter, so again I checked the OED, wondering if "retreat" had perhaps changed meaning since the 19th century. It has not. The only possible meanings in this context are and always have been, since the 1400s:

> **OED, definition of *retreat*, Entry#4:** (a) A place providing shelter or security; a refuge. (b) A place providing privacy or seclusion for the purposes of prayer, study, or meditation, or for rest and relaxation; a quiet or secluded dwelling or residence. (d) A hiding place.[19]

Therefore, a "retreat" has always been a safe and even restful place – an abode to which Jacob could happily descend, perhaps even to sup with the Pharisees. It is nothing at all like Wermullerus described *sheol*. In Strong's Concordance only the Greek *Gehenna*, which was used in the New Testament, is defined as the place of retribution:

Strong, Greek *Gehenna* (#1067): a valley of Jerusalem, used (fig.) as a name for the place (or state) of eternal punishment.

Thus Strong's definitions create a distinction between Sheol/Hades and Gehenna, making them two separate places. They also indicate that only the New Testament spoke expressly about hell, the place of eternal retribution. I then checked Strong's entries under "heaven," and discovered to my surprise that his definitions indicate also that only the New Testament spoke of heaven as "the abode of God" – and apparently God alone, since there is no mention of departed spirits:

Strong, Hebrew/Chaldee *shamayim, shamayin* (#8064, 8065): The *sky* (as *aloft*; the dual perh. alluding to the visible arch in which the clouds move, as well as to the higher ether where the celestial bodies revolve).

Strong, Greek *ooranos* (#3772): The *sky*, by extens. *heaven* (as the abode of God); by impl. *Happiness, power, eternity*; spec. the Gospel (Christianity).

How could the Hebrew lexicon omit any reference to heaven as the abode of God? It seems this could only have been an oversight, but how could such an oversight occur in so foundational a matter? And how then was it not overlooked in the Greek lexicon? In any case, Strong created several false impressions: (1) that just as the OT did not teach about hell, neither did it teach about heaven; (2) that there are two places beneath the earth where the dead go, one friendly and one a place of punishment; (3) that no one is in heaven in the interim state, but all are below in the abode called Sheol. The end result is that the traditional distinction between heaven and hell is destroyed, and there is a great deal of uncertainty concerning other questions.

Thayer's Greek-English Lexicon

Joseph Thayer authored his Lexicon in 1885, with a corrected edition in 1889, also during the time of preparation of the RV. The publisher's introduction to the 4th edition of Thayer's lexicon cautions the reader that "Thayer was a Unitarian.... The reader should be alert for both subtle and blatant denials of such doctrines as the Trinity [...and] the eternal punishment of the wicked." No doubt Thayer was a welcome voice on the RV revision committee.

Thayer's entries in his lexicon were often long, much more in the nature of a theological discourse than a definition. But perhaps this is to some extent inescapable when it comes to defining biblical terms – which highlights the risk to students who rely on the reference works of unbelievers. Thayer's definition of *hades* differed from Strong's. He described it as a "dark and dismal place in the very depths of the earth." He wrote that *hades* is "the common receptacle of disembodied spirits" (#86), but, in his definition of *ooranos*/heaven, opined that the Old Testament saints and Christians go to heaven after death. He explained, though somewhat ambiguously, that these saints and Christians will later be joined by virtuous dead people who will be raised from Hades after the Lord returns. Thayer also divided heaven into "several distinct heavens," but would not say who dwelt where in these various heavens:

> **Thayer on heaven (*ooranos*, #3772):** Several distinct heavens are spoken of also in Eph. iv.10; cf. Heb. vii.26, if it be not preferable here to understand the numerous regions or parts of the one and the same heaven where God dwells as referred to. The highest heaven is *the dwelling-place of God*....

> Into heaven have already been received the souls both of the OT saints and of departed Christians, Heb. xii.23, and heaven is appointed as the future abode of those who, raised from the dead and clothed with superior bodies, shall become partakers of the heavenly kingdom, 2Co. v.1, and enjoy the reward of proved virtue, Mt. v.12; Lk. vi.23. (Emphasis original)

Concerning questions about the existence and locality of *hades*, Thayer referred readers to a book by the 19th century author Edward Greswell. I consulted Greswell's book, and found that he cautioned his readers not to approach the doctrine of eternal retribution with "prejudices." He taught that Hades is (or would be, it was not clear to me) divided in two parts: one for the good, and *Gehenna* for the devil and the reprobate.[20] Greswell also asserted that the Psalmist David was in Hades.[21] However, since this contradicts Thayer himself, one wonders why Thayer referred the reader to him.

It is all quite contradictory and confusing, but in the end it tends to the same thing: to redefine *sheol* and *hades*, undermine or deny traditional doctrine, and leave the reader in a fog.

Girdlestone: Synonyms of the Old Testament and Modern Ideas

In 1871, the Hebrew scholar Robert B. Girdlestone published *Girdlestone's Synonyms of the Old Testament*.[22] A second edition followed in 1897. In his discussion of *sheol*, Girdlestone wrote, "Not in one single passage is [*sheol*] used in the sense of the place of punishment after the resurrection, concerning which little, if anything, is definitely revealed in the OT."(308) He said verses that had been traditionally linked with hell, which describe misery, suffering, and destruction, have to do only "with ordinary history, without at all referring to the destiny of the individual in any state of existence beyond this world."(298) In his subtly-worded introduction, he said, without actually saying so, that the "verdict" of the Scriptures concerning man's destiny after death is "smooth things," and this even despite "passages in the NT that point in another direction." (295) This, of course, is the Larger Hope.

Girdlestone was the head of the translation department of the British and Foreign Bible Society from 1877-1889. In 1887, only two years after the publication of the RV Old Testament, he published a small book entitled *How to Study the English Bible*.[23] In it he quickly passed over the history of previous translations of the Bible and concluded:

> Various attempts have been made to revise the Translation [i.e. the 1611 KJV] in later times, but none need be referred to here except the Revised Bible, which was issued in 1885. This Bible was prepared by companies of learned men of various Protestant denominations, and is of very great value, not only as a book of reference when we wish to know the literal meaning of the words of Scripture, especially in the Old Testament, but also for enabling the English reader to get a much clearer idea of the meaning of such books as Job in the Old Testament, and the Epistles in the New. (11)

Girdlestone closed chapter VI of his little book, which ostensibly dealt with doctrine, with the unorthodox admonition that when we read the Bible, "We must distinguish between the fate of the devil and the destiny of those whom he deceives." (96) Also, in his chapter on Christian doctrine, Girdlestone advised people to study ancient and heathen religions as part of their Christian education. (107) Pagan literature, regardless of the fact that it was demonically inspired, was a popular study among higher critics of the 19th century, who believed it might help them understand some of the concepts and semantics of the Bible.

Girdlestone also wrote a book entitled *Old Testament Theology and Modern Ideas*.[24] The title alone is a red flag, and the book confirms Girdlestone's unorthodoxy. He wrote:

> There is evidently hope, even for the most desperately wicked of natures ... We are sure that they will justify God in the day of visitation (Ps li,4), but we do not clearly see how. It is impossible to conceive that the patriarchs imagined men to be like the beasts that perish. They must have shared, to say the least, the current beliefs of Chaldea and Egypt in their time. The prophets taught that Death and Sheol were to be done away with (see Hos. xiii,14).... The Old Testament did not declare the whole truth.... As a system of theology, it is incomplete. (84-85)

This is an unbelieving soup of progressive revelation, universalism, higher criticism, and heathenism: imagine thinking that the patriarchs, chosen out of the world, shared the beliefs of the world. Girdlestone does not present Christ as the Messianic hope, but asserts that faith must be in "the known attributes of God," in his love and mercy – the pagan approach to God without Christ. He also asserts that there will be restitution for Sodom and Gomorrah. (86) This proves him a universalist and false teacher, whose work cannot be trusted.

THE REDEFINITION OF 'SHEOL' IN THE REVISED VERSION

Gesenius: Hebrew-Chaldee Lexicon and "shades of the dead"

H.W.F. Gesenius (1786-1842) was an influential German scholar and one of the early lights of higher criticism. He wrote *Gesenius' Hebrew-Chaldee Lexicon to the Old Testament*. The editor of his English edition warns the reader of Gesenius's "neologian" tendencies; that is, his novel and rationalistic views. Gesenius approached Hebrew by studying its historical development through the Semitic languages of heathen peoples. He did not ask, "What did the Hebrew say?" but, rather, "What might we understand from the etymology of the word, and from how other nations and religious groups used related words?" Like Girdlestone, he treated God's word as a natural book with shared heathen roots.

Gesenius's entry for *sheol* accords with the RV definition, though, like Thayer, he did not go as far as Strong, to portray *sheol* as a "retreat." He described it as "a subterranean place, full of thick darkness, in which the shades of the dead are gathered together" – whatever "shades of the dead" might be. In an explanatory note, Gesenius restricted the meaning "hell" to Syriac and Ethiopian usage, thus denying this meaning to the Hebrew. In a further note, he added that he had been impressed by an etymological study of the German words *holle, hohle,* and *hohl* (hell, cave, and hollow), and the German etymology led him to deduce that the Hebrew *sheol* meant no more than "a hollow and subterranean place." The fanciful and speculative nature of this ought to be obvious. In any case, Gesenius's work has been widely received, and informs modern Hebrew studies. I saw his influence in the RV, in a marginal note that referred to "shades of the dead."

Two schools of thought. The biblical evidence supports the traditional school.

Therefore, since the opening of the 20th century there have been two prominent schools of thought. One is the traditional school, which agrees more or less with Wermullerus. The other, the modern school, holds that *sheol* and *hades* do not denote the place of eternal punishment, and that the OT taught little if anything about this place. Remarkably, I have read commentators of the modern school who, influenced by the work of the RV revisers and academics, teach that David and the prophets of the Old Testament did not understand about hell (or heaven). This is the fruit of the RV transliteration of *sheol* combined with their re-definition and, also, the idea of progressive revelation.

But not only do modern transliterations and lexicons contribute to this view, so also do unclear translations of related biblical passages. Eternal retribution is inextricably tied in with the final judgement, so when verses concerning the judgement are obscured, it adds to the impression that the OT revealed little about these important things. The Geneva Bible is responsible for initially obscuring some such passages, of which the Ecclesiastes verse below is only one example. Since the GNV, it has never been clearly translated:

Ecclesiastes 3:17

MB God shall separate the righteous from the ungodly, and then shall be the time and judgement of all counsels and works.

GNV God will judge the just and the wicked: for time is there for every purpose and for every work.

THE REDEFINITION OF 'SHEOL' IN THE REVISED VERSION

KJV, RV God shall judge the righteous and the wicked: for there is a time there for every purpose and for every work.

NIV God will bring into judgement both the righteous and the wicked, for there will be a time for every activity, a time to judge every deed.

The NIV appears to refer to several judgements and links them somehow with activities.

However, the prophets spoke clearly about the judgement, as in the MB translation of Ecclesiastes 3:17, and in the books of Job and Daniel below. Daniel 12:2 is still intact in most modern versions:

Job 19:29, MB But beware of the sword, for the sword will be avenged of wickedness; and be sure, that there is a judgement.

Daniel 12:2, MB Many of them that sleep in the dust of the earth shall awake: some to the everlasting life, some to perpetual shame and reproof.

Further, the witness of the New Testament itself supports the traditional school. It is clear from the Gospels that teachings about the general resurrection, judgement, and hell, were known to the first century Jews. They could only have learned these things from the OT. Some of the Jews denied the doctrines; some believed; but all were aware. The Sadducees, who denied the resurrection and the afterlife, tried to trap Jesus with their question about the seven brothers who married one woman, but Jesus told them they did not understand the Scriptures or the power of God (M't 22:23-32). Martha, the sister of Lazarus, was wiser than the Sadducees; she believed her brother would rise again in the resurrection at the last day (Joh. 11:24). Further, when Jesus preached to the Jews, he spoke concerning hell and the judgement in terms that made it clear he assumed the people knew what he was talking about:

> **Matthew 12:42** The queen of the south will rise at the day of judgement with this generation and will condemn them, for she came from the furthermost parts of the world to hear the wisdom of Solomon, and behold, one greater than Solomon is here.

> **Mark 9:45-46** If your foot causes you to offend, cut it off. For it is better for you to go lame into life than, having two feet, to be cast into hell, into fire that never shall be quenched, where their worm dies not and the fire never goes out.

In Acts 24, the apostle Paul confirmed the widespread expectation of the Jews about the coming resurrection and judgement. Even non-believing Jews expected this judgement. The New Testament had not yet been written, and it is beyond question that the expectation of the Jews arose from Old Testament teaching. This must have included teaching about *sheol*. Paul's whole point was that the Jews expected the same resurrection and judgement that he did. Here is what he said, when the Jews accused him before Felix:

> **Acts 24:14-15** This I confess to you: that in accordance with the Way, which they call heresy, so do I worship the God of my fathers, believing all things that are written in the law and the prophets. And I have hope in God, that the same resurrection of the dead that they themselves look for also will come, both of the just and the unjust.

In Acts 24:25, we learn that when Paul spoke to Felix about the coming judgement, the ruler "trembled." It was not the *sheol* of the RV Old Testament, Jacob's abode, that made him tremble. Only the *sheol* of hell could have done that. The RV re-definition was wrong.

The re-definition of "sheol" undermines the gospel

The Scripture represents hell by different words (more on this in part 3). The RV revisers seized on this to say that there are *two* places below the earth, one an "abode" and the other a *Gehenna*. In addition to heaven, this makes three possible places, depending who you believe, where the spirits of the departed may go.

However, the gospel limits man's destiny to two places: hell below without God or heaven above with God. There is no third option. Hell is where man by nature goes, unless saved. Salvation is by Christ alone through faith, which opens the way to heaven. To add a second place outside of heaven where departed spirits may go, a place other than hell, suggests there is another criterion besides faith and believing on Christ that determines our destiny. As I pondered this, it struck me that this is a subtle denial of the Trinity. Believing *on* the Son of God means being *in* him, and *through* him entering into eternal life in the Trinity of the Father, Son, and Holy Spirit. For our life is hid with Christ in God (Col. 1:3), by whom we are made one with the Father, as Jesus did testify:

> **Excerpts from John 17, NMB** These words Jesus spoke, and lifted up his eyes to heaven and said, Father, the hour is come. Glorify your Son so that your Son may glorify you. For you have given him power over all flesh, so that he may

> give eternal life to as many as you have given him. This is life eternal: to know you, the only true God, and Jesus Christ whom you have sent...
>
> I have declared your name to the men that you gave me out of the world.... I pray not for them alone, but also for those who will believe on me through their preaching: that they all may be one, as you, Father, are in me, and I in you; that they may also be one in us.

This oneness with God is salvation, and it is found only in Christ, by whom we become partakers of the divine nature (2Pe. 1:4) by the power of the Holy Spirit. If we are not found in the oneness of the Trinity, we are lost. There is no place outside the Son to escape this fate. Granted there must be degrees of suffering in hell below, but that does not make two places of it, any more than it makes three, four, or five places of it.

It is a great mystery, but the only doctrine that makes consistent sense of the teaching of the Bible is the traditional doctrine of heaven and hell. Either we are saved, or we are lost. Either we know God through Christ, or we do not. Again, either we are dead in Adam, or alive with Christ (Ro. 5:17-18). In Adam all die, but in Christ, all are made alive (1Co. 15:22). Through the gospel God calls the sheep unto him, who then live with him through Christ. To be called unto him means that we will be with him. To be with him is to belong in heaven. Not be with him is to belong in hell. Thus there is heaven, and there is hell. Period.

The RV revisers said they would "introduce as few alterations as possible" into the biblical text, but this was deceptive. They said they would limit their alterations to the language of the KJV, but where it was of foundational importance, as with "hell," they did not. In their explanation for the alteration to "Sheol," they did not openly deny eternal retribution, but neither did they clearly affirm it. This omission must be construed against them. With everything else we have seen, it is evident that they considered the traditional doctrine of eternal retribution to be one of the "errors and prejudices" that should be quietly eliminated from the Scriptures, and they laboured diligently to that end.

PART THREE

The treatment of *sheol* in the 1537 Matthew Bible. Comparing the Geneva Bible, Revised Version, and modern Bibles.
The problems with the modern translations.

> Though there are several Scriptures which represent man as one being, namely, souls and body united, yet there are many other Scriptures ... wherein the souls and bodies of men are represented as two very distinct things. The one goes to the grave at death, and the other either into Abraham's bosom, or to a place of torment.
>
> – Isaac Watts

As DISCUSSED, UNTIL modern times *sheol* was often translated "hell" in the Old Testament of English Bibles, as well as "pit" and "grave." It was the only Hebrew word translated "hell," but other Hebrew words, such as *bore,* are also important: used in certain contexts, they round out the picture of *sheol* as 'hell.' In one sense, *bore* means a dungeon or pit in the earth where prisoners are held. In this use, it was sometimes a synonym for hell. For reasons best known to themselves – probably because it was not necessary to make "hell" disappear from the Old Testament – the RV revisers did not transliterate *bore.* Historically *bore* has been translated "pit" and "grave," and I also found "the deep" in the Matthew Bible. The Hebrew word *shakhath* was also translated "pit," as well as "destruction," "corruption," etc. *Shakhath* and words that indicated destruction or misery were sometimes used to flesh out a depiction of hell and the pit, as in Psalm 55:23 ("The pit of destruction," Heb. *bore* and *shakhath*), and Proverbs 15:11 ("Hell and her pain are before the Lord," Heb. *sheol* and *abaddon*). In the New Testament, *Gehenna*, a powerful figure of evil and suffering, and *tartaroo*, indicating casting into a dungeon, are used as well as *hades* with reference to hell.

I went through the Old Testament in the Matthew Bible and reviewed every use of *sheol*, the word on which so much depends. Rogers added several explanatory notes throughout, from which two things emerge. First, *sheol* had a variety of meanings, and second, the abode of all departed spirits is not one of them. Jacob is not in *sheol*. However, Rogers' notes explain that *sheol* was indeed used generically at times in the Old Testament; that is, with reference to all people, not just with reference to the wicked or to the place of eternal torment. The failure to distinguish generic from particular uses appears to have misled the RV revisers; or, at least, it provided occasion for them to improperly define the word. Depending on the context, according to Rogers' notes in the Matthew Bible, *sheol* might mean:

1. The place of torment beneath the earth, where evil people go after they die; that is, hell itself. This particular sense was well understood in 1537, as it is now.

2. Figuratively, the evils and afflictions of hell or the power of the devil. In expressions like "the sorrows of hell," it may refer to the afflictions suffered by evil

people in hell beneath, or generically to the afflictions that both good and evil people suffer in this life; for until the Lord returns, the devil still has power on earth (under God).

3. In a broad, generic sense, *sheol* means the grave or pit where the bodies of all people go when they die. This may include the ocean deep, which is the grave of sailors lost at sea. Figuratively in this sense, *sheol* indicates the common death, through which all people must pass, or the condition or estate of death.

Uses in the first sense hardly required an explanation. Rogers did clarify who is in hell:

Psalm 6:5 MB In death no man remembereth thee; O who will give thee thanks *in the hell*?

*MB note: They be in death and in hell who dispraise and blaspheme God, as it is said Psalm .cxv.

You will not find a single note to this effect in the Revised Version of the Bible. Later we will see how other Bibles have handled this verse.

Rogers' main concern was to explain the generic and figurative uses of *sheol* in the OT, which are potentially the greatest source of confusion. In the Psalm below, Rogers explained the second sense of *sheol* carefully, so people would not think King David feared going to hell:

Psalm 18:4-5 MB The sorrows of death compassed me, and the brooks of ungodliness made me afraid. The *pains of hell* came about me; the snares of death took hold upon me.

*MB note: By the sorrows of death and brooks of ungodliness (by which is meant the obstinate multitude of the wicked and ungodly), the *pains of hell*, and the snares of death, are signified the jeopardous and terrible fears which, by the wickedness of his enemies, happened to him, and brought him very often even to death's door, so that by the judgement of the flesh he thought himself utterly cast away.

As to the third sense of *sheol*, Rogers explained in a note on Jonah 2:2, "The Scripture speaketh of hell [*sheol*] commonly as of a place common for all them that go down into the earth, as into a grave or into the deep of the sea, etc., as ye have in Genesis and in the Psalms." This was the sense in the Genesis passages where Jacob spoke of "going to the grave." Another use is in Psalm 30 below; however, Coverdale translated "hell" here, and since this might lead readers to think that King David feared going to the place of the wicked, Rogers clarified the generic sense:

Psalm 30:2-3 MB O Lord my God, I cried unto thee, and thou hast healed me. Thou Lord hast *brought my soul out of *hell*; thou hast kept my life, whereas they go down to the pit.

*MB note: Here it is manifest that hell is taken for the estate of the dead, as well of the good as of the evil, as it is said in Genesis 37:35.

In Psalm 30, the GNV and KJV revised to "grave." In my view this was an appropriate revision, because it better suggests that David was referring to the common death. However, there were places where the context indicated hell itself, and in those places it was misleading to substitute "grave," as we shall now see.

Misleading translations in the GNV as well as the RV

The charts in part 2 showed that, in the Old Testament, the RV had 70% fewer mentions of "hell" than the MB, but also that the 1599 GNV had 58% fewer mentions. Both versions reduced mention by over half. As discussed, the RV revisers often substituted "grave" or "Sheol" for "hell," and then changed the meaning to the abode of departed spirits. However, the puritan scholars in Geneva also substituted "grave" for "hell," and then changed the meaning in their own way. Their meaning, which we will have a closer look at in this part, was the common death and corruption of the body. This was an effective re-definition that also suppressed the teaching of hell. Further, their new focus suggested the common death, not hell, is man's chief danger. A glaring example is in the book of Job:

Job 26:6

MB All *they which dwell beneath in the hell* are not hid from him, and the very destruction itself cannot be kept out of his sight.

GNV *The grave is* [1]*naked* before him, and there is no covering for [2]*destruction*.

GNV note 1: There is nothing hid in the bottom of the earth but he seeth it.

GNV note 2: Meaning, the grave wherein things putrify.

KJV *Hell is naked* before him, and destruction has no covering.

RV [1]*Sheol is naked* before him, and Abaddon has no covering.

RV note 1: Or, *The grave.*

In Coverdale's translation it is clear that hell is a real place with dwellers or inhabitants. However, the change to "grave" in the GNV changed the imagery and the meaning.[25] Note 2 then limited the application of the verse to "things" (not spirits) that "putrify" (that is, which produce a foul smell when they rot). This ignores hell and the soul. Note 1 also referred to things ("nothing"). The GNV thus made it impossible to understand this verse as a literal reference to *sheol*/hell as a real place with real inhabitants.

In Proverb 15:11, the GNV was first again to defeat a clear and simple teaching of *sheol* as 'hell.' The translation "hell" was kept, but the notes present it as a metaphor – as if hell is not a real place, but just a figure or metaphor of the Lord's all-seeing eye:

Proverbs 15:11

MB The hell with her pain is known unto the Lord; how much more then the hearts of men?

GNV [1]Hell and destruction are before the Lord; how much more the hearts of the sons of men?

***GNV note 1:** There is nothing so deep or secret that can be hid from the eyes of God, much less man's thoughts.

RV [1]Sheol and [2]Abaddon are before the Lord: how much more then the hearts of the children of men!

***RV note 1:** Or, *The grave.*

***RV note 2:** Or, *Destruction.*

The GNV note on Proverbs 15:11 is false, even though what it says is true. It is false because it wrongly changed the meaning.

If hell is a real place, this verse needed no note. It simply meant what it says: hell and its suffering are known to the Lord. But the GNV taught that the verse means that everything is known to the Lord. While this is true, to treat hell as a metaphor for this truth implicitly denies its reality. The RV also denied hell by referring to "Sheol" and "the grave."

In Psalm 49 below, King David was rejoicing in his soul's deliverance from hell. However, the GNV revision to "grave" wrongly suggests that David was referring to deliverance from the bodily death. Certainly there is a time and place for that rejoicing (see Isaiah 38 below); however, here again it is wrong, because the context is the soul and eternal salvation. Rogers gave the context in his chapter summary:

Psalm 49:15

Chapter summary, MB: The misery and madness of them that set by riches, who receive their felicity in this world, and shall after continually remain in hell: whereas the virtuous shall have everlasting joy.

MB God shall deliver my soul from the *power of hell, when he receiveth me.

***MB note:** That is, from perdition and eternal damnation.

GNV God shall deliver my soul from the power of the grave, *for he will receive me.

***GNV note:** Or, because he has received me.

RV God will redeem my soul from the *power of Sheol.

***RV note:** Heb. *hand.*

The Matthew Bible presents hell as a danger to man's soul, but the GNV presents the grave as a danger to the soul. It might be argued that this use was figurative, but there was no need for a figure here, much less a figure of the common, bodily death. Further, the GNV suggests David would be delivered from the grave. He would not, and the apostles emphasized in their preaching that he died and was buried in a grave (Ac. 2:29, 13:36).

In the next example the GNV and RV both kept "hell," but used their notes to divert the focus to the grave:

Isaiah 5:14

MB Therefore gapeth hell, and openeth her mouth marvelous wide, that pride, boasting, and wisdom, with such as rejoice therein, may descend into it.

GNV Therefore [1]hell has enlarged itself, and has opened his mouth without measure, and their glory, and their multitude, and their pomp, and he that rejoiceth among them, shall descend into it.

*GNV note 1: Meaning, the grave shall swallow up them that shall die for hunger and thirst, and yet for all this great destruction it shall ever [sic] be satiate.

RV Therefore [1]hell has enlarged her desire, and opened her mouth without measure: and their glory, and their multitude, and their [2]pomp, and he that rejoiceth among them, descend into it.

*RV note 1: Or, *the grave* Heb. *Sheol.* See Gen. xxxvii.35.

*RV note 2: Or, *tumult.*

After deflecting focus to the grave, the GNV note speaks of bodily death from hunger and thirst, ignoring the soul's eternal punishment for pride, etc. Though prior verses indeed referred to hunger and thirst, the GNV note defeated the true meaning of this verse by suggesting it referred only to the physical death. The RV re-definition is also troublesome: *sheol*/hell/the grave is revealed as an undesirable place where the wicked go, but if it is where the patriarch Jacob is, then it appears that he dwells with the pompous multitude. The RV notes do nothing to resolve this dilemma.

The new meanings in the GNV and RV were too persistent, and too similar in consequence, to be inadvertent or coincidental. Both versions suppressed the knowledge of the existence and reality of hell. This strongly indicates that the same spirit guided them both. Other inappropriate revisions in the GNV included Psalm 16:10, where the translation was changed from "Thou shalt not leave my soul in hell" to "Thou wilt not leave my soul in the grave." Again, it is confusing to suggest that souls go to the grave. In Psalm 55:15, an imprecation against the wicked was changed from "Let them go down quick into hell" to "Let them go down quick into the grave," as if their destiny and punishment is the physical death, not hell. The King James Version restored "hell" in these places, but many moderns have substituted "grave," as the GNV had, or "realm of the dead," which is the core definition of the RV. Does this not indicate that the same spirit has also guided the modern revisions, even if the translators are unaware? Step by subtle step, and with increasing boldness, hell has been removed from the Old Testament.

The denial of hell is no new thing

In a note in the Matthew Bible, Rogers made a pertinent argument about the suppression of the doctrine of hell in the Old Testament. In Isaiah 38, the righteous King Hezekiah, who had been sick but was miraculously healed, said he had feared "the gates of hell [*sheol*]." Rogers explained that he meant this in the generic sense: the king had feared an untimely death. Rogers also added a complaint against certain heretics who denied that hell even existed in the Old Testament age:

> **Isaiah 38:10 MB** I thought I should have **gone to the gates of hell* in my best age, and have wanted [been deprived of] the residue of my years.
>
> ***MB note:** That is, I thought I should have gone to my grave and died in my best age, etc. The Hebrew word [*sheol*] signifieth both hell and a grove, pit, or ditch. Ye may perceive this in Genesis 42:38, where Jacob says that if any misfortune should happen to Benjamin in his journey into Egypt with his other brethren, his grey head would be brought with sorrow unto his grave. Here the common translation readeth "hell" for "grave." As for Hezekiah, he neither feared hell nor purgatory, as ye may well see in that a little before he says, "Remember O Lord that I have walked before thee in truth and a steadfast heart, and have done the thing that is pleasant to thee." Which thing, whosoever doeth it need not to fear any of those two places. Besides that, the Duns men and sophisters themselves, who were (as most learned men think) the inventors and devisers, yea and the very makers of purgatory, say that before the time of Christ's coming there was no such place.

Therefore, Hezekiah is by their judgement free and quit of that place. And the word of God doth acquit him of hell, which says there is no condemnation to them that are in Christ Jesus. Romans 8 A.[26]

Thus there was no chance that the righteous king would descend to pass endless days with the pompous multitude.

Rogers' reference to Duns men and sophisters needs an explanation. These were Roman Catholic scholastics who, with their subtle philosophical disputations, destroyed the simplicity of the faith and devised many heresies. The early English Reformers rejected their teaching. Since many scholastics were followers of a medieval Scottish priest named John Duns, the term "Duns men" arose. (It was often written "dunce men" in English Reformation writings, whence the unflattering term "dunce.") The Duns men, like the RV men and higher critics, denied that the concept of hell belonged in the Old Testament. Further, some also shared a sympathy for the doctrine of purgatory. The same old heresies just keep resurfacing to plague Christendom!

"Hell" in the Old Testament: From 1537 to the present

For an overview of what has happened to the translation of *sheol* over the centuries, I tracked all 31 instances in the Old Testament where, according to Strong's Concordance, the KJV translated *sheol* as "hell," and then checked to see what other Bibles have done. The chart below shows that the transliteration "Sheol" has been adopted by several modern mainstream versions. (Note, the numbers do not match up with the charts in part 2 because they deal with different data):

Comparing translations of *sheol* in Bible versions.
Limited to verses where the KJV translated *sheol* by "hell."

Bible version	Hell	Grave	Pit	Sheol	Place/realm world of dead	Other *
MB	30		1			
GNV	20	11				
KJV	31					
RV	13		3	15		
NKJV	17			13		1
LB	15	1		1	1	13
NIV	0	5			17	9
NASB	0			31		
CJB	0			30		1
NLT	0	19			5	7
ESV	0			31		

* Other translations include "death," "the dead," "the depths," "underworld," "netherworld," and "devil."

Thus many modern Old Testaments do not mention "hell" at all, including the ESV, which has been adopted by many churches. Along with the influence of modern reference texts, it is no wonder people today do not believe the OT taught anything about hell – the very situation Rogers decried in his note on the Duns men. The NIV generally preferred "realm of the dead" to translate *sheol*, but since this is the RV re-definition, it appears that Hort's quiet process has come to full fruition in that version.

COMPARING THE MATTHEW BIBLE AND LATER VERSIONS

Following is a comparison of three verses from each of the Old and New Testaments, showing their translation since the Reformation. These examples reveal tendencies that we have already seen in the GNV: they either made a metaphor of that which the MB made literal,[27] or they changed the metaphor. An example of the latter is in Psalm 86:13 below. Here Rogers explained the figurative sense of *sheol*, so that it would not appear that David was in danger of the hell beneath. The GNV also gave a figurative sense, but again the grave is a different metaphor, and the teaching differs:

Psalm 86:13

MB For great is thy mercy toward me; thou hast delivered my soul from *the nethermost hell*.

*MB note: That is, out of extreme jeopardies.

GNV For great is thy mercy toward me, and thou hast delivered my soul from *the lowest grave*.

*GNV note: That is, from most great danger of death: out of the which none but only the almighty hand of God could deliver him.

KJV For great is thy mercy toward me: and thou hast delivered my soul from *the lowest hell*.

RV For great is thy mercy toward me; And thou hast delivered my soul from *the lowest pit*.

*RV note: Or, Sheol beneath.

NIV For great is your love toward me; you have delivered me *from the depths, from the realm of the dead*.

ESV For great is your steadfast love toward me; you have delivered my soul from the *depths of Sheol*.

The GNV again presents the common death, signified by the grave, as man's great danger; indeed, as his "most great danger." The RV note is also again troublesome because Sheol/the pit is presented as the last place David would want to be, yet previous notes indicate that Jacob is there. In the ESV, the capitalization of "Sheol" destroys any possibility of deriving a figurative sense.

In Psalm 6:5 below, the Matthew Bible brought clarity to the translation of *sheol*, so that the faithful need not be confused by the idea that after death they will not praise God. The Geneva Bible ignored the concept of hell:

Psalm 6:5

MB In death no man remembereth thee; O who will give thee thanks *in the hell*?

***MB note:** They be in death and in hell who dispraise and blaspheme God, as it is said Psalm .cxv.

GNV In death there is no remembrance of thee: *in the grave*, who shall praise thee?

***GNV note:** He lamenteth that occasion should be taken from him to praise God in the congregation.

KJV In death there is no remembrance of thee: *in the grave*, who shall give thee thanks?

RV For in death there is no remembrance of thee: *in Sheol* who shall give thee thanks?

***RV note:** See Gen. 37:35.

NIV Among the dead no one proclaims your name. Who praises you *from the grave*?

ESV For in death there is no remembrance of you; *in Sheol* who will give you praise?

According to the RV and ESV, Jacob is not praising God in Sheol.

In Proverbs 15:24 below, the ways of heaven and hell are compared. The MB unambiguously depicted heaven as the true reward of following the way of life, but the GNV presents the "way on high" as metaphor for the moral high ground. This subtly denies, or ignores, the reality of heaven above:

Proverbs 15:24

MB The way of life *leadeth unto heaven*, that a man should beware of *hell beneath*.

GNV The way of life *is on high* to the prudent, to avoid from *hell beneath*.

KJV The way of life *is above* to the wise, that he may depart from *hell beneath*.

RV To the wise the way of life *goeth upward*, that he may depart from **Sheol beneath*.

*RV note: Or, the grave.

NIV The path of life *leads upward* for the prudent to keep them from going *down to the realm of the dead*.

ESV The path of life *leads upward* for the prudent, that he may turn away from *Sheol beneath*.

The many revisions to the Old Testament over the years have changed the meanings of *sheol* and have undermined the traditional doctrine. The Matthew Bible alone presents it clearly and unambiguously.

"Hell" in the New Testament

As mentioned, most modern Bibles have not entirely removed references to hell in the New Testament. However, silence in the OT followed by references to hell in the NT supports the doctrine of progressive revelation and the teaching of the Duns men. Also, the mixed use of the words "Hades" and "hell" suggests that they are separate places, as Greswell taught – which, of course, was the point. Keeping "hell" in the New Testament, therefore, has not precluded significant changes in meaning. Another semantic twist can be seen in the RV and ESV below. The new translation, arising from a reinterpretation of the genitive case, says the danger is not of hell, but of fire. This suggests the fire of purgatory:

Matthew 5:22

MB Whosoever says, Thou fool, shall be in danger of *hell fire*.

GNV Whosoever shall say, Fool, shall be worthy to be punished with *hell fire*.

KJV Whosoever shall say, Fool, shall be worthy to be punished with *hell fire*.

RV Whosoever shall say, Thou fool, shall be in danger [1]of the [2]hell of fire.

*RV note 1: Gr. *Unto* or *into*.

*RV note 2: Gr. Gehenna of fire.

NIV Anyone who says, 'You fool!' will be in danger of *the fire of hell*.

ESV Whoever says, 'You fool!' will be liable to *the hell of fire*.

No textual variant that I found accounts for the new meaning in the RV and ESV.

The Geneva Bible had two notes on Matthew 5:22. I omitted them above, because they are unpleasant and distracting. However, they show what the puritan scholars did to New Testament, not to mention how unpleasantly they must have distracted 16th century readers, so I give them below:

> **M't 5:22, GNV** Whosoever shall say, Fool, shall be worthy to be punished with [1]*hell* [2]*fire*.
>
> ***GNV note 1:** Whereas we read here, Hell, it is in the text itself, Gehenna, which is an Hebrew word made of two, and is as much to say, as the Valley of Hinnom, which otherwise the Hebrews called Tophet: it was a place where the Israelites were wont most cruelly to sacrifice their children to false gods, whereupon it was taken for a place appointed to torment the reprobates in Jer. 7:31.
>
> ***GNV note 2:** The Jews used four kinds of punishments, before their government was taken away by Herod, hanging, heading, stoning, and burning: this is it that [which] Christ shot at, because burning was the greatest punishment, therefore in that he maketh mention of a judgment, a council, and a fire, he showeth that some sins are worse than other sins, but yet they are all such that we must give account for them, and will be punished for them.

These notes reveal (as shown in detail in *Story Part 2*) the unsettling, punitive focus of the Geneva Bible. The notes were an indirect justification for the burnings, beheadings, and cruel punishments and persecutions meted out in Geneva under

Consistory rule. Later in England, during the puritan revolution and rogue Parliament, there was more of the same. Also, in Massachusetts, where the puritans brought their Geneva Bible, there were hangings, burnings, ducking stools, and other punishments that I cringe to mention. It is sobering to consider how the GNV contributed to such atrocities – and also to think that, for the majority of people in the 16th century, this was their introduction to God's word, and to the gospel of mercy and forgiveness that is in Christ our Lord. It is not an exaggeration to say that, when the true history of the puritans is known and understood (again, as explained in *Story Part 2*), it becomes clear that, although their Bible made a metaphor of the hell that is below the earth, it contributed to making hell a reality upon the earth.

A GNV note on Revelation 20 below is also disturbing. It indicates that the dead, (even the "repugnant"!) do not live again (to serve God?) until the general resurrection. It strongly suggests a belief that the soul does not endure conscious and alive after the physical death – which would explain the frequent changes from "hell" to "grave" in the Geneva version. The Matthew Bible translation was closely followed in the GNV and KJV, so I will not repeat the translations, but show significant revisions in {special brackets}. English updates are in [square brackets]:

Revelation 20:11-15

MB, GNV, KJV 11 And I saw a great white seat {G,K throne} and him {G one} that sat on it, from whose face fled away both the earth and heaven, and their place was no more found {K and there was found no place for them}.

12 And I saw the dead, both great and small, stand before God. And the books were opened; and another book was opened, which is the book of life, and the dead were judged [by] those things which were written in the books according to their deeds {G,K works}.

13 ^{G1}And the sea gave up her dead, [who] were in her, *and death and hell delivered up the dead [who] were in them*, and they were judged every man according to his deeds {G,K their works}.

14 ^{G2}And death and hell were cast into the lake of fire. This is the second death.

15 And *whosoever was not* found written in the book of life was cast into the lake of fire.

MB: No note.

*GNV note 1: This is a prevention or an answer to an objection; for haply [perhaps] some man will say, but they are dead, whom the sea, death, and the grave has consumed. How shall they appear before the judge? S. John answereth by resurrection from death, whereunto all things (however repugnant) shall minister and serve at the commandment of God, as Dan. 12.

*GNV note 2: The last enemy which is death shall be abolished by Christ (that he may no more make any attempt against us) 1Cor. 15:16, and death shall feed upon the reprobate in hell forevermore, according to the righteous judgement of God, in the next verse.

The GNV does speak of eternal torment here, but the concept of "death feeding on the reprobate" is not meaningful English. To show how moderns handled Revelation 20, I will give only the last two verses. One of the chief differences between the RV and ESV as opposed to other Bibles is the change to the conditional mood in verse 15: *if* anyone was not found written in the book of life, as opposed to the indicative mood, *whoever* was not found written there. The second sentence in verse 14 reveals a manuscript difference in the Alexandrian manuscripts, which could be significant, depending how one interprets it:

Revelation 20:14-15

RV And death and Hades were cast into the lake of fire. This is the second death, even the lake of fire. And *if any was not found* written in the book of life, he was cast into the lake of fire.

NIV Then death and Hades were thrown into the lake of fire. The lake of fire is the second death. *Anyone whose name was not found* written in the book of life was thrown into the lake of fire.

ESV Then Death and Hades were thrown into the lake of fire. This is the second death, the lake of fire. And *if anyone's name was not found* written in the book of life, he was thrown into the lake of fire.

In the next and final example, the Reformation Bibles referred to "hell," but the GNV and KJV changed it. In the RV and modern versions, the new wording is due to a textual variant; in the RT the Greek was *hades,* but not in the Alexandrian manuscripts. This served the cause of the Larger Hope and could help explain the RV revisers' preference for the Alexandrian texts:

1 Corinthians 15:55

MB Death, where is thy sting? *Hell,* where is thy victory?

GNV O death, where is thy sting? O *grave*, where is thy victory?

KJV O death, where is thy sting? O *grave*, where is thy victory?

RV O death, where is thy victory? O *death*, where is thy sting?

NIV Where, O death, is your victory? Where, O *death*, is your sting?

ESV O death, where is your victory? O *death*, where is your sting?

Only the Matthew Bible teaches that the Messiah was victorious over *hell*.

Conclusion

The Matthew Bible taught clearly, in both the Old and New Testaments, about the general resurrection, the judgement, and hell. Only the Matthew Bible gave full heed to the grave out of which we have been dug. Beginning with the Geneva Bible, and continuing in great measure after the RV, the teachings were destroyed. The present situation, and the state of modern Bibles, entails serious consequences:

(1) The transliteration and re-definition of *sheol* and *hades*, along with the new treatment of *Gehenna*, resurrects the doctrine of the Duns men, that hell did not exist in the Old Testament age. Further, no longer does the Bible teach about heaven and hell; it posits two abodes beneath the earth, so that it teaches about

three places altogether: heaven, Sheol/Hades, and hell. The new translations enable universalism, annihilationism, and purgatory, which attack the foundation of the gospel: if man is not in danger of hell, what need is there of the salvation that is in Christ? Nothing is more important than man's eternal destiny, but modern Bibles do not teach truly about it.

(2) The new transliterations have created massive confusion. In a recent Facebook thread, someone said *hades* is a "paradise" where the Old Testament saints are waiting for Christ to come and take them to heaven. Depending who you read or consult, *hades* is a paradise, a retreat, an abode, a dark and dismal place, or hell itself. Anything is possible.

(3) Though the unbelievers and unrepentant may mock the fear of hell, it is a prod and a goad to the faithful, who, traversing the narrow and difficult road to heaven, do battle with the flesh and the devil. The fear of the Lord is the beginning of wisdom (Pr. 9:10). The wise fear his judgements. This fear needs to be clearly taught, even if only the faithful will give it heed, just as they alone give heed to the gospel – and rejoice in their salvation. The author of the Hebrews wrote that the doctrine of eternal judgement is foundational to the faith, and belongs to "the beginning of a Christian life" (Heb. 6:2).

(4) The problems with modern Hebrew and Greek reference texts call for cautious reliance on them. The risk of misleading earnest Bible students, who are often trying to make sense of obscure translations, is great. How much better to simply have a clear Bible and a few trusted expositors? Ideally, that would mean the Matthew Bible and the best of the Church fathers and early (pre-Geneva) Reformation writings.

(5) This brings me to the next point: modern Bibles have changed the language of the faith, which makes traditional resources less accessible. But, of course, that was the purpose.

(6) Taking the concept of hell out of the Old Testament severs doctrinal unity between the Testaments and makes the OT less relevant. It creates an internal inconsistency in the Bible, as we saw with Paul's testimony before Felix in Acts 24: if the OT did not teach about hell, then the passage makes no sense. It also contributes to the error of progressive revelation.

However, we can truly say that one thing has advanced progressively: the suppression, not the revelation, of the knowledge of the coming judgement and of eternal retribution. This *suppression* has advanced steadily since we received the Matthew Bible in the Reformation. The incremental revisions to the Scriptures, new commentaries, and the influence of higher criticism, have gradually brought us to the state that Tyndale foresaw would prevail at the end of the age:

> **William Tyndale, prologue upon 2 Peter. As updated in the October Testament:** In the latter days, the people, through unbelief and lack of fear of the judgement of the last day, will be even as Epicures, wholly given to the flesh. Which last day shall yet surely and shortly come, he says; for a thousand years and one day is with God the same thing. And he shows also how terrible that day will be, and how suddenly it will come. Therefore he exhorts all to look earnestly for it, and to prepare themselves for it with holy conduct and living.

Tyndale summed up the wisdom of the truth, and of the godly fear of the judgement. This fear was faithfully taught in the

Matthew Bible. However, the Geneva Bible taught the wrong fear, and the RV revisers and their associates, who preached the Larger Hope, denied that fear has any place in Christian doctrine.

> *Let us leave the questions that belong to the beginning of a Christian life, and let us go on to maturity, and not now again lay the foundation of repentance from dead works, and of faith toward God, of baptism, of doctrine, and of laying on of hands, and of resurrection from death, and of eternal judgment. (Hebrews 6:1-2)*

ENDNOTES

[1] I note that William Tyndale was not convinced of the conscious state of believers after the first death. He thought it possible that they rest in a literal sleep, and would not commit to a firm position. He was quite alone among the Reformers with this view.

[2] The final casting into hell with the demons must be the time the demons themselves referred to in Matthew 8:29, when they asked Jesus if he had come to torment them before the time was come.

[3] Quotations from the RV are from my original 1895 Oxford University Press edition.

[4] Theodore P. Letis, "The Quest for the Historical Text," a lecture delivered at the Van Andel Museum Center, Grand Rapids, Michigan, on May 16, 2003. Viewed on YouTube. Letis explains how this quest, disguised as textual criticism, originated as a quest to disprove orthodox Christian doctrine.

[5] Brooke Foss Westcott, *History of the English Bible,* 2nd ed. (London: MacMillan and Co., 1872), 134. See also *The Story of the Matthew Bible: That Which We First Received* (*Story Part 1*), chapter one and note 15 (pages 33-34 in the print edition). Moderns also say the RT was "corrupt." In 1964 Bruce Metzger published *The Text of the New Testament: Its Transmission, Corruption, and Restoration.* Letis (see preceding note) shows how textual criticism was used to try to prove that passages in the RT that affirm doctrines such as the Trinity (such as the Johannine comma) were later additions to, and therefore "corruptions of," the text. By this means they would reveal those doctrines as unchristian. Many previously devout persons, such as Sir Isaac Newton, were led to disavow the Trinity after investigating textual criticism. However, to those who have eyes to see, there are many other passages in the New Testament that affirm the Trinity and the divinity of Christ.

[6] See chapter 3 of *The Story of the Matthew Bible: The Scriptures Then and Now* (*Story Part 2*). See also Dennis Kenaga, *Skeptical Trends in New*

Testament Textual Criticism: Inside the Alexandrian Priority, www.all-of-grace.org/pub/kenaga/SkepticalTrends.pdf, 3. Kenaga estimates that less than 1% of textual variants have any real significance.

[7] For Greek text comparisons, for the Received Text I use the *Greek Text New Testament* set by Stephen Austin and Sons for the Trinitarian Bible Society in 1976, which was based on *The New Testament in the Original Greek According to the Text Followed in the Authorized Version,* edited by F. Scrivener and published 1894-1902, as set forth in Green, *Interlinear Bible, Hebrew, Greek, English,* 2nd edition (USA: Hendrickson Publishers, 1986). For Critical Text Bibles I use the *Nestle Greek New Testament* of Eberhard Nestle, which was based on Westcott and Hort along with two others, as set forth in Zondervan's *Interlinear KJV-NIV Parallel New Testament in Greek and English,* ed. Alfred Marshall (Michigan: Zondervan Publishing House, 1975).

[8] Fenton Hort, from *The Life and Letters of F. J. A. Hort,* Vol. I, 400, as cited in Benjamin Wilkinson, *Our Authorized Bible Vindicated* (Washington, D.C.: No pub., 1930), 160.

[9] These guiding principles are given in the OT and NT prefaces to the RV.

[10] The universalist Samuel Cox rejoiced that the RV supported universalism, and asserted that Westcott and Hort believed in the Larger Hope, per Samuel C. Gipp, *An Understandable History,* see note 12. Also, Westcott is identified as sympathetic with the Larger Hope by Thomas Allin in *Christ Triumphant: Universalism Asserted as the Hope of the Gospel on the Authority of Reason, the Fathers, and Holy Scriptures* (Oregon: Wipf & Stock Publishers, 2015), 190. Viewed on Google books.

[11] *Life of Hort,* Vol. I, 118, as cited at https://heritagebbc.com/wp-content/uploads/2018/02/Views-Complete-4a-and-b.pdf). Accessed January 2020.

[12] As quoted in Samuel C. Gipp, *An Understandable History of the Bible,* chapter 8, posted at https://www.eaec.org/bibleversions/understandable_history_bible/08.htm.

ENDNOTES

[13] B. F. Westcott, *Some Lessons of the Revised Version of the New Testament*, 196, as cited in Wilkinson, *Vindicated*, 196.

[14] Calvin's words from his commentary on Jeremiah 31, one of the most important prophecies of the New Covenant, were, "God has never made any other covenant than that which he made formerly with Abraham, and at length confirmed by the hand of Moses... Let us now see why he promises to the people a new covenant. It being new, no doubt refers to what they call the form; and the form, or manner, regards not words only, but first Christ, then the grace of the Holy Spirit, and the whole external way of teaching." (Discussed in *Story Part 2*.) Calvin opposes Luther. See paper posted on Academia.edu, www.academia.edu/41932368/Luther_ vs._Calvin _on_the_New_Covenant.

[15] Hort, *The Apocalypse of St. John*, 4, as cited in Wilkinson, *Vindicated*, 197.

[16] B. F. Westcott, from *Life and Letters of Brooke Foss Westcott*, Vol. I, 78, as cited in David Blunt, "From Their Own Mouths – Westcott and Hort," at https://savedbygrace.com/bible/mouths-westcott-hort.

[17] Vance Smith, *Bible and Theology*, 281, as cited in Wilkinson, *Vindicated*, 197-98.

[18] *OED online*, s.v. "abode." See entry 4.

[19] Ibid., s.v. "retreat."

[20] Edward Greswell, *An Exposition of the Parables and Other Parts of the Gospels* (Oxford: J.G.&F. Rivington, 1835), 364. Viewed on Amazon.com by the look inside feature. Greswell's lengthy, wandering, sometimes self-contradictory chapter X, which Thayer referenced specifically in his entry on *hades*, was entitled "On the Existence and Locality of Hades." He emphasized that all souls go to *hades*: the good go down to one part, and the bad to another (366).

[21] Ibid., 285.

[22] Robert B. Girdlestone, *Girdlestone's Synonyms of the Old Testament*, 3rd ed. (MI: Baker Book House, no date). Girdlestone said the translation "nether world" might have been better than the transliteration "Sheol." Some modern Bibles now use "nether world." Girdlestone believed that the account of the rich man and Lazarus shows the rich man is not in hell but in Sheol/Hades, which he believes is separate from hell (see p.308). Chapter 24 of Girdlestone's book contains his unorthodox discussion of death and hell.

[23] Girdlestone, *How to Study the English Bible* (London: The Religious Tract Society, 1887). Viewed on https://issuu.com/theologyontheweb/docs/how-to-study-the-english-bible_gird.

[24] Girdlestone, *Old Testament Theology and Modern Ideas* (London: Longmans, Green and Co., 1909). Viewed at https://issuu.com/theologyontheweb/docs/old-testament-theology_girdlestone.

[25] The Great Bible, the base of Geneva version, had "hell," but did not refer to dwellers as such.

[26] Quotation updated (syntax, subjunctive, also obsolete words: "finder" to "deviser," "sentence" to "judgement" or omitted, "dunce men" to "Duns men," "skilled" to "free and quit").

[27] *Story Part 2* reveals, in their own words, how Calvin and the Geneva Bible revisers made metaphors of Messianic prophecy. See chapter 14 especially. Also briefly discussed in my blog post at www.baruchhousepublishing.com/calvin-on-prophecy-30-pieces-of-silver. Also discussed in *The Judaizing Calvin*, written by 16th century Lutheran theologian, Aegidius Hunnius.

www.ingramcontent.com/pod-product-compliance
Lightning Source LLC
Chambersburg PA
CBHW020906080526
44589CB00011B/469